PHILIPPIANS

LIFE IN CHRIST

STUDY GUIDE

LECTIO

UNVEILING SCRIPTURE AND TRADITION

TIM GRAY

Nihil Obstat: Alphonso L. Pinto, STD, *Censor Deputatus*
Imprimatur: Most Reverend Samuel J. Aquila, S.T.L., Archbishop of Denver, March 2018

Copyright © 2018 Augustine Institute. All rights reserved.
With the exception of short excerpts used in articles and critical reviews, no part of this work may be reproduced, transmitted, or stored in any form whatsoever, printed or electronic, without the prior permission of the publisher.

Some Scripture verses contained herein are from the Catholic Edition of the Revised Standard Version of the Bible, copyright ©1965, 1966 by the Division of Christian Educators of the National Council of the Churches of Christ in the United States of America. Used by permission. All rights reserved.

English translation of the *Catechism of the Catholic Church* for the United States of America, copyright ©1994, United States Catholic Conference, Inc.—Libreria Editrice Vaticana. English translation of the *Catechism of the Catholic Church*: Modifications from the Editio Typica copyright ©1997, United States Catholic Conference, Inc.—Libreria Editrice Vaticana.

Writers: Ashley Crane, Kris Gray, Cathy Loh

Media: Steve Flanigan, Justin Leddick, Kevin Mallory, Ted Mast, Jon Ervin, Matthew Krekeler

Print Production/Graphic Design: Jeff Cole, Brenda Kraft, Jane Myers, Christina Gray, Ann Diaz, Julia DeLapp

Augustine Institute
6160 South Syracuse Way, Suite 310
Greenwood Village, CO 80111
AugustineInstitute.org/programs
(866) 767-3155
AugustineInstitute.org/lectio

Printed in the United States of America
ISBN 978-0-9982041-5-4

(Cover Art) St. Paul the apostle writing an epistle, by P. Sacchi. © Restored Traditions. Used by permission.

TABLE OF CONTENTS

PHILIPPIANS
Life in Christ

Welcome to Lectio 1

Session 1: Paul and the Philippians 3

Session 2: Partnership in the Gospel 19

Session 3: Friendship in Christ 35

Session 4: The Mind of Christ 53

Session 5: Imitatio Christi 69

Session 6: All Things in Christ 85

LECTIO

UNVEILING SCRIPTURE AND TRADITION

What Is LECTIO?

To read is to discover meaning from written symbols or text. Letters form into words, words into sentences, and sentences into whole paragraphs and pages that communicate our thoughts, teach new ideas, and narrate stories that we find amusing, sorrowful, imaginative, or deeply profound.

The Latin term *lectio* means "reading." The tradition of reading Sacred Scripture for prayer and reflection was practiced by many of the early Church Fathers—St. Ambrose, St. Jerome, St. Augustine, St. Cyprian, and St. John Chrysostom, just to name a few. Benedictine monks later developed this practice into the tradition known as *lectio divina*, or "divine reading."

Lectio uses the practice of prayerful reading and study to help us dive more deeply into the truths of the Faith and discover the profound meaning and purpose of Sacred Scripture, Sacred Tradition, and Church History. We combine engaging sessions led by Catholic teachers with practical guidance for living the Faith and developing the disciplines of reading, reflecting, and responding.

By prayerfully reading and understanding the texts of Sacred Scripture and Tradition, we can come to discover the story of salvation into which our Baptism has united us, the history of God's people through the centuries, and the depth of God's love for each of us.

Welcome to Lectio

Welcome to the Lectio Study Series. In these sessions of Lectio you will discover the profound importance, meaning, purpose, and beauty of Sacred Scripture and Sacred Tradition, as seen through the eyes of the Church.

Lectio studies are designed for adult faith formation to help unveil both Sacred Scripture and Sacred Tradition. The Latin word *lectio* means "reading," and often refers to a careful and prayerful reading of Scripture. These studies cover a wide variety of topics, including individual books or letters of the Bible, the lives and writings of the saints, Church teaching, and topics to help serve the formation of Catholics living out the call of the New Evangelization.

A Lectio Session

This Study Guide takes you step by step through each session, both the small group gathering and video teaching, as well as five days of personal follow-up study. The resources are carefully crafted to lead you through an opening of your heart and mind to God's Word and the Traditions of the Catholic Church.

What You'll Find in Each Lectio Session:

CONNECT

1. **Opening Prayer:** For this study on St. Paul's Letter to the Philippians, we have chosen the Prayer to the Apostle St. Paul for the Jubilee Year of St. Paul (2008-2009).

2. **Introduction:** We begin with a brief overview of the topic, including the key points for the session. This helps contextualize the topic, show its relevance for daily life, and inspire you to delve into a particular aspect of the Faith.

3. **CONNECT Questions:** After reviewing the memory verse and daily reflections from the previous session, you'll share your thoughts on questions related to the new session.

VIDEO

4. **Video Teaching:** The video segments present teaching that delves into and makes relevant the Sacred Scripture and Sacred Tradition of the Catholic Church. The video teachings for the study on Philippians are presented by Dr. Tim Gray, President of the Augustine Institute. The Study Guide includes a brief outline of the key points in the teaching.

DISCUSS

5. **DISCUSS Questions:** Each video segment is followed by questions that will help you personalize and take ownership of the topics of the session.

6. **Memory Verse:** The Psalms encourage us to treasure God's Word in our heart through memorization, saying, "I have laid up thy word in my heart . . ." (Psalm 119:11). You are encouraged to memorize and reflect on a Scripture verse for every session to help nurture your faith.

7. **Closing Prayer:** The Closing Prayer has been chosen to reflect back to God an appropriate response to his loving action in the session.

8. **For Further Reading:** For supplemental study, you are encouraged to refer to the additional reading resources.

9. **Quotes, Tips, and Definitions:** We have included throughout the study interesting quotes and excerpts from saints, Catholic documents, the *Catechism of the Catholic Church*, and Catholic authors to enhance your understanding of each topic.

COMMIT

The Study Guide includes five daily COMMIT reflections that will help you more deeply explore the main topics of each session and more firmly commit to following Christ in your daily life. These reflections include more information on Sacred Tradition and Sacred Scripture, as well as topics such as geography, history, and art. Some of these reflections will also include times of prayer, including the practice of Scripture meditation known as *lectio divina*.

An Overview of Lectio Divina

Lectio divina is an ancient practice of enhancing one's prayer life through the power of God's Word. The term itself means "divine reading" of the Sacred Scriptures. It is our hope that by using these simple steps each day as you study Sacred Scripture in Lectio, you will develop an effective way to study and pray with God's Word and hear God's voice in your daily life.

- **Sacred Reading of the Scriptures *(lectio):*** The reading and rereading of the Scripture passage, paying close attention to words, details, themes, and patterns that speak to you.

- **Meditation *(meditatio):*** Meditating or reflecting on what you've read to gain understanding. Allow the Holy Spirit to guide you as you spend time pondering what you have read and striving to understand it in meditation.

- **Prayer *(oratio):*** A time to bring your meditative thoughts to God in prayer. Talking with God about how the connections and implications of your meditation on the Scripture affect your life and the lives of those around you.

- **Contemplation *(contemplatio):*** A time of quiet and rest, we listen and await God's voice. Contemplation allows one to enter decisively and more deeply into the mystery of God— this is no small endeavor, so be patient as you engage this step and strive to be receptive to God's voice speaking into your life.

- **Resolution *(resolutio):*** A call for resolution and action, inviting you to respond to the things you have read in Scripture and have prayed about and to put them into practice.

To learn more about *lectio divina*, refer to Dr. Tim Gray's *Lectio: Prayer* study, available at www.augustineinstitute.org/programs, or his book, *Praying Scripture for a Change*, available at www.AscensionPress.com.

SESSION 1

Paul and the Philippians

Opening Prayer

Glorious Saint Paul,
Most zealous apostle,
Martyr for the love of Christ,
Give us a deep faith,
A steadfast hope,
A burning love for our Lord,
So that we can proclaim with you,
"It is no longer I who live,
But Christ who lives in me."

Help us to become apostles,
Serving the Church with a pure heart,
Witnesses to her truth and beauty
Amidst the darkness of our days.
With you we praise God our Father:
"To him be the glory, in the Church
And in Christ,
Now and forever."
Amen.

—Prayer to the Apostle St. Paul,
for the Jubilee Year of St. Paul (2008–2009)

Introduction

St. Paul's Letter to the Philippians may be short, but it packs a powerful punch. Many may already be familiar with its popular verses such as "Rejoice in the Lord always" (Philippians 4:4) and "I can do all things in him who strengthens me" (Philippians 4:13). But other treasures of this epistle include the model it provides for working together in partnership to advance the Gospel, the beautiful relationship of mutual love that unites Paul and the church in Philippi, and Paul's great hymn to Christ in Philippians 2:6–11. This first session begins by looking at the town of Philippi, its first converts, and Paul's opening words to them in his epistle.

St. Paul the apostle writing an epistle by P. Sacchi.
© Restored Traditions. Used by permission.

Connect

How often do you think about your citizenship? How important is it to you?

Which sounds like a stronger statement: "I feel like this is important" or "I think that this is important"? Why?

Video

Watch the video segment. Use the outline below to follow along and take notes.

I. Paul's Letter to the Philippians
   A. Short, tightly written gem
   B. Written toward end of Paul's life
   C. Philippi
      1. Macedonian Roman colony
      2. Via Egnatia (Roman road)
      3. Philippians support Paul in prison
      4. Close relationship between Paul and Philippians
   D. Themes in letter
      1. Joy and friendship
      2. Citizenship—privileges and rights; key to identity
      3. Paul redirects Greek ideals in light of Christ
      4. Poem/hymn for Christ

II. Greeting—Philippians 1:1–2
   A. Letter writer(s): Paul and Timothy
   B. Servants (*douloi*)—slaves
   C. To the saints (*hagioi*) in Christ Jesus
   D. With bishops (*episkopoi*) and deacons (*diakonoi*)
   E. Grace and Peace
      1. Peace (*shalom*)—fruit of God's blessing; fruit of Holy Spirit
      2. Grace—Paul changes *chairein* (health and well-being) to *charis* (grace)

SESSION 1

PAUL AND THE PHILIPPIANS

III. Opening Prayer of Thanksgiving—Philippians 1:3–11
   A. Takes up Paul's hope and concerns for this community
   B. Thanks (*eucharistein*)
   C. Joy used throughout the letter
   D. Partnership (*koinonia*)
   E. Greek *phronein* (to "think"); separation/distinction of head and heart is not current in Paul's day/thought

DISCUSS

1. What was one thing you heard for the first time or that was an "aha" moment for you?

2. What does Paul's greeting to the Philippians tell us about his relationship with them? How does this greeting prepare us to better understand the rest of the letter?

3. What is different about Paul's use of common words and ideas like *citizenship*, *peace*, *grace*, and *friendship*? What does his particular use of these words accomplish in his letter?

MEMORY VERSE

"I am sure that he who began a good work in you will bring it to completion at the day of Jesus Christ."
—Philippians 1:6

CLOSING PRAYER

Lord Jesus Christ, Son of the Father,
we thank you for the gift of your grace and peace.
Give us the strength to be faithful to the Gospel
with which you have entrusted us.
May we persevere in joy and obedience,
confident that you will bring to completion your good work in us.
All glory and praise to you, Lord Jesus Christ.
Amen.

FOR FURTHER READING

Dennis Hamm, SJ, *Philippians, Colossians, Philemon* (Baker Academic: 2013)

Commit—Day 1
Philippi

Setting sail therefore from Troas, we made a direct voyage to Samothrace, and the following day to Neapolis, and from there to Philippi, which is the leading city of the district of Macedonia, and a Roman colony.

—Acts 16:11–12a

Map of Greece © pavalena / shutterstock.com

Ancient amphitheater in the archeological area of Philippi, Eastern Macedonia © stoyanh / shutterstock.com

Philippi was a Roman colony in eastern Macedonia (northern Greece), situated about ten miles inland from the seaport of Neapolis (modern Kavala). Philippi was founded by colonists from the island of Thasos around 360 BC and originally named Krenides (from the Greek word for "spring") because of the abundant sources of fresh water. A few years later the city was conquered by Philip II of Macedon, the father of Alexander the Great. Philip fortified the city, added additional settlers, and renamed it after himself. Today it is still possible to view the remains of city walls built by Philip II, a theatre likely built by Philip and renovated in the second and third centuries AD, remains of two Roman bathhouses, the agora or Roman forum, a temple dedicated to the cult of the emperor, and an aqueduct.

Running through Philippi was the Via Egnatia, a road constructed by the Roman senator Gnaeus Egnatius in the mid-second century BC. It stretched almost 700 miles from Dyrrhachium (modern Durrës) on the Adriatic Sea in the west to Byzantium (later called Constantinople, now Istanbul) in the east. It ran through parts of what is now Albania, the Republic of Macedonia, Greece, and Turkey.

Roman road Egnatia, near Kavala, Greece © vlas200 / shutterstock.com

The Via Egnatia, like other Roman roads, was about six meters (almost twenty feet) wide and paved with large stone slabs or covered with packed sand. These major arteries stretched from one end of the empire to the other and allowed the transport of trade goods, armies, officials, civilians, and postal communication. As part of this system, the Via Egnatia was essentially a continuation of the Via Appia, the road to Rome—the Via Appia ended on the west coast of the Adriatic Sea at Brundisium, and directly across the sea the Via Egnatia began at Dyrrhachium and continued east. Because of Philippi's location on the Via Egnatia, the second-century historian Appian of Alexandria called it "the gate from Europe to Asia."

St. Paul travels the Via Egnatia from Philippi to Thessalonica on his second missionary journey (see Acts 17:1). Other famous travelers of the road include the armies of Julius Caesar and Pompey during Caesar's civil war, Mark Antony, Octavian, Cassius, and Brutus prior to the Battle of Philippi, and emperor Trajan and his armies in his campaign against the Parthians in the early second century AD. By the fifth century AD, the road saw decreased use, due in large part to the growing violence and instability in the region.

In 42 BC, Philippi was the site of the decisive Roman civil war battle between Brutus and Cassius (the assassins of Julius Caesar) and Mark Antony and Octavian (better known by his later title of Caesar Augustus). Mark Antony and Octavian defeated Brutus and Cassius on the plains west of the city. After the Battle of Philippi, the city was elevated to the rank of Roman colony, and many Roman army veterans were settled there. As a colony, Philippi was considered a satellite city of Rome. Colonies were subject to the imperial laws of Rome rather than their own local laws; they had a particular duty to behave like a loyal outpost of Rome and possessed special privileges that other cities and territories did not. The residents of Philippi associated very closely with Rome—they were not Philippians living under Roman rule; they were Romans living in Philippi.

Read Philippians 3:20. In light of Philippi's status as a Roman colony and the large population of Roman citizens living there, what is the significance of Paul reminding the Christians that their "commonwealth" (or citizenship) is in Heaven?

_____

_____

_____

We too often need to hear Paul's reminder in our own lives. How does the world distract us from the truth that our commonwealth and citizenship is first and foremost in Heaven?

_____

_____

_____

Writing to the Colossians, Paul exhorts, "Set your minds on things that are above, not on things that are on earth" (Colossians 3:2). At various moments during the liturgical year, the Church echoes this exhortation in her prayers, reminding us that, as we walk amid passing things, our participation in the sacramental mysteries, especially the Eucharist, teaches us to love the things of Heaven and hold fast to what endures. Participating often in the sacraments is one way to keep our focus on our heavenly citizenship.

Commit—Day 2
Paul and the Philippians

Paul first visits Philippi in AD 49 or 50 during his second missionary journey. Philippi is not Paul's first choice of destination—from Phrygia and Galatia he originally tries to enter the province of Asia, but the Holy Spirit had other plans. When Paul arrives at the Aegean port of Troas, he has a dream in which he sees a man pleading with him to come to Macedonia (see Acts 16:6–10).

Paul and his companions (Silas—Acts 15:40; Timothy—Acts 16:3; and Luke—Acts 16:10) sail to Neapolis and travel from there to Philippi along the Via Egnatia. Paul's strategy in each new city is to start in the synagogue and preach the Gospel to the Jewish community (see Acts 17:1–2, 18:1–4, for example). However, since there is not a large Jewish community in Philippi, there is no synagogue. As a result, Paul goes to the river outside the city on the Sabbath (see Acts 16:13). Running water was considered clean, and so in the absence of a synagogue Jews would gather by a river or stream as a place for prayer and worship.

At the river, Paul finds a group of women, including Lydia, a righteous Gentile. When Lydia hears the message of the Gospel, she immediately asks to be baptized, and she welcomes Paul and his companions into her home. She is Paul's first European convert to Christianity, and her house becomes the home of the church in Philippi.

St. Lydia, the first documented convert to Christianity, and it was by St. Paul © Restored Traditions. Used by permission.

God-fearer

Acts 16:14 describes Lydia as "a worshiper of God" or a God-fearer. This title was used for Gentiles who embraced Judaism and followed many of its moral laws. They believed in the one true God and prayed and worshipped with the Jewish community, but they were not full converts to Judaism because they did not receive circumcision. Another prominent God-fearer in the early Church was the centurion Cornelius, "a devout man who feared God with all his household, gave alms liberally to the people, and prayed constantly to God" (Acts 10:2). The Holy Spirit sent Peter to preach the Gospel to Cornelius and his household, and these God-fearers were the first Gentile converts to Christianity.

Unfortunately, not everyone in Philippi responds well to Paul's work there. Read Acts 16:16–34. How do Paul and Silas end up in trouble in Philippi? How are they rescued?

_____

_____

SESSION 1 — PAUL AND THE PHILLIPIANS

Now compare the arrest of Paul and Silas in Acts 16:20–24 with their release in 16:35–39. Why do you think Paul says nothing about their citizenship when they are accused, but brings it up when they are released?

_____

_____

In hindsight, it seems that Paul and Silas could have avoided a great deal of suffering if they had only claimed the protection of their Roman citizenship when they were first accused before the magistrates. They didn't use their citizenship to avoid their own suffering, but Paul demanded a public apology so that there would be no scandal surrounding him to cast a shadow over the new church in Philippi.

After their release, Paul and Silas leave Philippi and continue on to Thessalonica, apparently leaving Luke behind with the new Philippian converts (compare the "we" in Acts 16:10–17 with the "they" in Acts 16:40 and 17:1). Paul visits Philippi again during his third missionary journey, where Luke rejoins him in his travels (see Acts 20:3–6).

In his letter Paul calls the Philippians his "joy and crown" (Philippians 4:1). The converts who so readily welcomed the message of the Gospel would continue to "shine as lights in the world" (Philippians 2:15).

Greece, archeological area of ancient Philippi © fritz16 / shutterstock.com

Troas and the New Empire of Rome

The Roman poet Virgil's masterpiece the *Aeneid* tells the epic legend of Aeneas, who fled the ruined city of Troy and traveled west to establish his family in Italy, becoming the ancestor of Romulus and Remus—the founders of the city of Rome. Written early in the reign of Caesar Augustus, the *Aeneid* provided a masterful narrative supporting the legitimacy of Augustus's rule and his vision of renewing the greatness of Rome.

Acts 16:11 states that Paul and his companions sailed from Troas, a seaport only miles from ancient Troy, to travel west bearing the Good News of the Kingdom of God. Eventually both Peter and Paul travel to, and are martyred in, Rome and, as a result, come to be seen as the twin founders of a new Christian Rome. When writing The Acts of the Apostles, St. Luke, an educated Greek physician familiar with Greco-Roman history and literature, includes the seemingly trivial detail about Paul's point of departure for his journey to the Roman colony of Philippi and in doing so begins the reworking of the defining narrative about Roman identity so as to point to the universal sovereignty of the Gospel.

Commit — Day 3
Lectio: Philippians 1:1–2

Nearly all ancient Greco-Roman letters followed a standard structure. The opening of a letter often consisted of a simple identification and greeting: "Writer, to recipient, greetings." This would be followed by a brief wish or prayer for the well-being of the recipient. Paul follows this basic structure in his letters, but he makes it uniquely his own—his combination of traditional Greek and Hebrew greetings carry the added weight of the divine subject matter and eternal significance of his correspondence.

> **LECTIO:** The practice of praying with Scripture, *lectio divina*, begins with an active and close reading of the Scripture passage. Read the verse below and then answer the questions to take a closer look at some of the details of the passage.

Paul and Timothy, servants of Christ Jesus, To all the saints in Christ Jesus who are at Philippi, with the bishops and deacons: Grace to you and peace from God our Father and the Lord Jesus Christ.
—Philippians 1:1–2

Who is writing? How are they described?

_____
_____

To whom is the letter addressed? How are they described?

_____
_____

What does the author wish for the recipients of the letter?

_____
_____

> **MEDITATIO:** *Lectio*, a close reading and rereading of Scripture, is followed by *meditatio*, a time to reflect on the Scripture passage, and to ponder the reason for particular events, descriptions, details, phrases, and even echoes from other Scripture passages that were noticed during *lectio*. Take some time now to mediate on the above verse.

SESSION 1

PAUL AND THE PHILLIPIANS

From the Second Vatican Council document, *Lumen Gentium*, speaking about the universal call to holiness:

> The Lord Jesus, the divine Teacher and Model of all perfection, preached holiness of life to each and everyone of His disciples of every condition. He Himself stands as the author and consumator of this holiness of life: 'Be you therefore perfect, even as your heavenly Father is perfect.' Indeed He sent the Holy Spirit upon all men that He might move them inwardly to love God with their whole heart and their whole soul, with all their mind and all their strength and that they might love each other as Christ loves them. The followers of Christ are called by God, not because of their works, but according to His own purpose and grace. They are justified in the Lord Jesus, because in the baptism of faith they truly become sons of God and sharers in the divine nature. In this way they are really made holy. Then too, by God's gift, they must hold on to and complete in their lives this holiness they have received. They are warned by the Apostle to live "as becomes saints" and to put on "as God's chosen ones, holy and beloved a heart of mercy, kindness, humility, meekness, patience," and to possess the fruit of the Spirit in holiness. Since truly we all offend in many things we all need God's mercies continually and we all must daily pray: "Forgive us our debts."
>
> Thus it is evident to everyone, that all the faithful of Christ of whatever rank or status, are called to the fullness of the Christian life and to the perfection of charity; by this holiness as such a more human manner of living is promoted in this earthly society. In order that the faithful may reach this perfection, they must use their strength accordingly as they have received it, as a gift from Christ. They must follow in His footsteps and conform themselves to His image seeking the will of the Father in all things. They must devote themselves with all their being to the glory of God and the service of their neighbor. In this way, the holiness of the People of God will grow into an abundant harvest of good, as is admirably shown by the life of so many saints in Church history.
>
> —*Lumen Gentium*, 40

What does it mean for Paul and Timothy to identify themselves as servants or slaves *(duloi)* of Christ Jesus? Can we use that term to describe ourselves?

_____

_____

_____

How does Paul's use of "all" when addressing the saints *(hagioi)* point to the universal call to holiness?

_____

_____

_____

SESSION 1

PAUL AND THE PHILIPPIANS

What does Paul's use of "our" in "God our Father" tell us about how we can answer the call to holiness?

_____

_____

_____

> **ORATIO, CONTEMPLATIO, RESOLUTIO:** Having read and meditated on today's Scripture passage, take some time to pray, bringing your thoughts to God (*oratio*) and and to be receptive to God's grace in silence (*contemplatio*). Then end your prayer by making a simple concrete resolution (*resolutio*) to respond to God's prompting of your heart in today's prayer.

_____

_____

Meditative Paul at a table in his prison cell, holding a writing quill by Rembrandt
© *Everett-Art / shutterstock.com*

Commit – Day 4
Mind and Heart

What would you say is more important: how you feel about something or what you think about it? Modern western society largely takes the distinction between the mind and the heart for granted. And when the two are pitted against each other, emotions often come out as the winner in the modern view: "Follow your heart. Don't overthink things," is common advice. If someone simply *thinks* something is true, you can try to talk him or her out of it. But if that person *feels* very strongly about something, that's likely to be the end of the conversation.

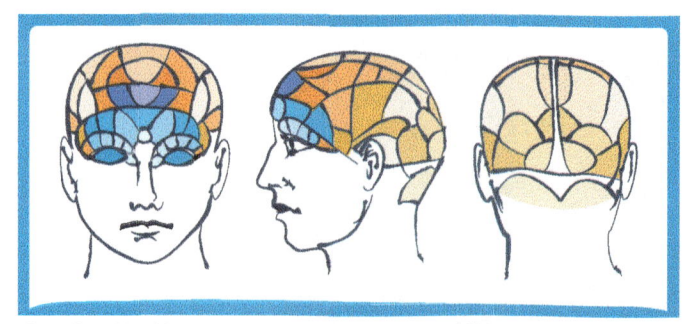

Phrenology. Head brain map. Infographic.(c) Polina Kudelkina / shutterstock.com

The eighteenth-century intellectual movement known as the Enlightenment was characterized by a focus on the supremacy of reason. This led to a distinction between the rational mind as the seat of thought and decision and the irrational heart as the source of emotion. There can be a wide chasm between thinking and feeling, and although this separation originally grew out of an emphasis on the mind, it has turned upside down and often results in a tyranny of feelings over reason.

In what ways have you witnessed the separation of mind and heart play out in your own life? In society? What potential consequences does this tyranny of feelings have?

_____

_____

But for most of history, this was not the case. Many ancient cultures—including those of Egypt, Mesopotamia, Babylon, and India—considered the heart to be the seat not only of emotion but of reason. And so for Paul, writing from his Hebrew theological background as well as the first-century Greco-Roman culture in which he lived, our modern separation between the head and the heart did not exist.

A bright, red heart and gray brain sit on opposite ends © Mark Carrel / shutterstock.com

SESSION 1

PAUL AND THE PHILIPPIANS

Phronein

The Greek word *phronein* means "to have a certain mindset." It is often translated "to think," but it refers to an entire attitude or outlook, not just to a single thought. This is the verb Paul uses in Philippians 1:7 when he is talking about being thankful for the partnership of the Philippians (verse 5) and his confidence that God will complete his good work in them (verse 6). The RSV translates *phronein* in verse 7 as "It is right for me to *feel* this way about you all" (emphasis added), but Paul is talking about his mindset toward the Philippians, not his emotions about them.

Paul doesn't just feel happy about the Philippians, as some modern translations might lead us to think. In the original Greek he says that he thinks (*phronein*) joyfully about them (see Philippians 1:7). When he goes on to say that he holds them in his heart, he is not talking about a mere feeling of love and friendship—although the letter makes it clear that he holds great affection for the Philippians—but rather about the depth and intimacy of his relationship with them.

Look up the following verses. What do they say about the heart?

Deuteronomy 6:4–7 _____

Jeremiah 31:33 _____

Ezekiel 36:26–27_____

Matthew 6:19–21 _____

Luke 8:15_____

Romans 5:5_____

Based on these verses, how would you describe the biblical understanding of the heart? Considering St. Paul's background as a scholar of the Law and Scriptures, what do you think he means when he says he holds the Philippians in his heart?

_____

_____

> *"Keep your heart with all vigilance; for from it flow the springs of life."*
> —Proverbs 4:23

Commit – Day 5
Truth and Beauty

St. Paul Writing – Pier Francesco Sacchi, c. 1520, National Gallery, London

St. Paul the apostle writing an epistle by P. Sacchi. © Restored Traditions. Used by permission.

Pier Francesco Sacchi was a painter of the Genoese guild during the early sixteenth century. While only a few paintings can be attributed to him, they are all of religious subjects, such as his *Parting of St. John the Baptist from his Parents* (Oratory of St. Maria at Genoa), *Crucifixion with Saints* (Berlin Museum), and *The Four Doctors of the Church* (Louvre Museum). In *St. Paul Writing*, Sacchi depicts Paul writing one of his many letters recorded for us in the New Testament.

SESSION 1

PAUL AND THE PHILIPPIANS

As a painter, Sacchi has been described as having a lively interest in accessories, landscape, costume, and details, sometimes to the point of excess. We see such details here, but each is put to good use. Paul's small table, supported by a scrolled pedestal, is crowded with a few necessary items, including his ink well, prayer book, and crucifix. But these few items are finely detailed—the prayer book with its closing strap and markers, the crucifix with its base relief, and the shapely ink well. At the heart of these items, Paul writes on a slanted easel whose sides display an ornately carved scene of playful cherubs. Paul holds a reed pen in one hand, ready to begin his next sentence. In the other hand, he holds his knife, ready for trimming his reed or cutting the paper when his letter is complete. Leaning against the writing desk is a sword, its long handle beautifully decorated and engraved. St. Paul is depicted with his characteristic long beard. His trimmed blue tunic is overlaid with a vibrant red cloak, its color, along with the sword, a reminder of the death he will suffer for his witness to Christ.

If we look out the room's rear window, we see a detailed landscape with a city sitting along a hillside. Nearby are a river and woods, with mountains in the distance. In this scene is a solitary traveler walking along a path, knapsack over his shoulder, approaching a bridge by which he can make his way to the town and its people. The scene reminds the viewer of the many miles that St. Paul traveled on his various missionary journeys throughout Asian minor, Macedonia, and Greece. Like the traveler, Paul walked countless miles in order to preach the Gospel, and then to later return and strengthen the Christian communities that developed among those who heard his preaching and believed in Jesus Christ.

But these many details and accessories cannot keep the viewer from the central focus of the painting: Paul's intense gaze upon the Cross of Christ. Look up the following verses. What does Paul have to say about the Cross of Christ?

1 Corinthians 1:17–23 _____

1 Corinthians 2:2 _____

Galatians 2:20_____

Galatians 6:14_____

Ephesians 2:13–18_____

Benedict XVI, in one of his General Audiences during the Pauline Jubilee Year, beautifully describes this focus of St. Paul:

> In [Paul's] encounter with Jesus the central significance of the Cross had been made clear to him: he understood that Jesus *had died and rose for all* and for himself [Paul]. Both these things were important; universality: Jesus really died for all, and subjectivity: he also died for me. Thus God's freely given and merciful love had been made manifest in the Cross. Paul experienced this love in himself first of all (cf. Gal 2:20) and from being a sinner he became a believer, from a persecutor an apostle. Day after day, in his new life, he experienced that salvation was "grace", that everything derived from the death of Christ and not from his own merit, which moreover did not exist. The "Gospel of grace" thus

17

became for him the only way of understanding the Cross, not only the criterion of his new existence but also his response to those who questioned him . . . For St Paul the Cross has a fundamental primacy in the history of humanity; it represents the focal point of his theology because to say "Cross" is to say *salvation* as grace given to every creature.
—Benedict XVI, General Audience, October 29, 2008

Interestingly, Sacchi's painting show Paul as he writes the beautiful chapter on love from his First Epistle to the Corinthians. Sacchi gives us the moment just after Paul writes, "Love is patient and kind; love is not jealous or boastful . . ." (1 Corinthians 13:4). The Apostle who desired to boast in nothing but the Cross of our Lord Jesus pauses, his eyes fixed on him who is the model of the love he is describing. Paul gazes upon the crucifix, upon him who "humbled himself and became obedient unto death, even death on a cross" (Philippians 2:8), all so that Paul (and each of us) might be reconciled to God (see Romans 5:1–10) and spend eternity in the embrace of this love.

Take a moment to journal your ideas, questions, or insights about this lesson. Write down thoughts you had that may not have been mentioned in the text or the discussion questions. List any personal applications you got from the lessons. What challenged you the most in the teachings? How might you turn what you've learned into specific action?

_____
_____
_____
_____
_____
_____
_____
_____
_____
_____
_____
_____

SESSION 2

PARTNERSHIP IN THE GOSPEL

OPENING PRAYER

Glorious Saint Paul,
Most zealous apostle,
Martyr for the love of Christ,
Give us a deep faith,
A steadfast hope,
A burning love for our Lord,
So that we can proclaim with you,
"It is no longer I who live,
But Christ who lives in me."

Help us to become apostles,
Serving the Church with a pure heart,
Witnesses to her truth and beauty
Amidst the darkness of our days.
With you we praise God our Father:
"To him be the glory, in the Church
And in Christ,
Now and forever."
Amen.

—Prayer to the Apostle St. Paul,
for the Jubilee Year of St. Paul (2008–2009)

INTRODUCTION

In the last session we looked at the background for St. Paul's Letter to the Philippians and its opening verses. In this session we will explore Paul's circumstances as he writes this letter under house arrest in Rome. We will also look more closely at the relationship between Paul and the Philippians, what Paul describes as their *koinonia*, or "partnership." This partnership, with its risks and its rewards, is something into which we are invited to enter as well.

The Basilica of St. Paul Outside the Walls is one of the four papal basilicas of Rome © salvo77_na / shutterstock.com

Connect

When have you had to rely on a partnership with someone to accomplish a goal? How did the partnership help accomplish the goal? How did you feel about not being solely responsible for the outcome?

Describe a time when something that initially seemed like a limitation or setback actually opened the door to new opportunities.

Video

Watch the video segment. Use the outline below to follow along and take notes.

I. Review
   A. Paul writing from prison but joyful
   B. Paul reaps what he sowed (in Acts)
   C. Paradox of announcing Good News while in chains

II. Opening Prayer—Philippians 1:7
   A. Partakers (*koinonia*)
      1. More business partnership than fellowship
      2. Paul intensifies: *syn-koinonia*—"with" partnership
   B. Paul and Philippians in venture *together*
   C. Kingdom of God is a venture to save souls

III. Opening Prayer—Philippians 1:8–11
   A. Paul calling in witnesses because he is on trial
   B. Mind and heart are to work together
   C. "Love . . . with knowledge and all discernment"
   D. Approve (*dokimazo*)—to test, think through, calculate
   E. Moral life leads to the liturgical life; life lived well gives glory

SESSION 2　　　　　　　　　　　　　　　　　　　　　　　PARTNERSHIP IN THE GOSPEL

IV. Current Events—Philippians 1:12
   A. Paul's difficulty leads to others advancing the Gospel
   B. Paul's fearlessness makes others bold
   C. Defense (*apologia*) of the Gospel (not of Paul)
   D. Paul's abandonment to God's Providence
   E. Paul quoting Job 13:16; innocent, yet suffers

DISCUSS

1. What was one thing you heard for the first time or that was an "aha" moment for you?

2. Why does St. Paul pair "love" with "all knowledge and discernment"? What are some consequences of separating love from knowledge and discernment?

3. What is the connection between the moral life and the liturgical life for Paul? How do you see this connection in your own experience?

4. St. Paul relates how his imprisonment made many other brethren "much more bold to speak the word of God without fear" (Philippians 1:14). What causes this courage? How do the lives of the saints encourage you in your daily walk with Christ?

SESSION 2   PARTNERSHIP IN THE GOSPEL

MEMORY VERSE

"It is my prayer that your love may abound more and more, with knowledge and all discernment, so that you may approve what is excellent." —Philippians 1:9–10

CLOSING PRAYER

Heavenly Father,
teach us to rejoice in your will no matter the cost,
as your Apostle St. Paul did.
May we be completely devoted to the work of the Gospel
and dedicated to the glory of your name.
Let our love abound more and more,
with knowledge and all discernment.
Teach us to approve what is excellent,
that we may be pure and blameless for the day of Christ.
Fill us with the fruits of righteousness, which come through Jesus Christ.
We ask this in his name.
Amen.

FOR FURTHER READING

Pope Benedict XVI, *Saint Paul* (Ignatius Press: 2009)

Commit – Day 1
Paul in Prison

The Letter to the Philippians has such a joyful, victorious tone—making it easy to forget that St. Paul wrote this letter under rather dire circumstances. In fact, Paul doesn't even get around to mentioning his own circumstances until verse 12. Instead, his first words speak of his gratitude to God and the joy and hope he finds in the church at Philippi. It's only after this initial greeting and prayer for his beloved Philippians that Paul talks about his imprisonment.

This imprisonment that Paul mentions in Philippians 1:13 is by no means the first imprisonment Paul has endured, but it is the last one explicitly mentioned in Scripture. In fact, the Acts of the Apostles closes

Meditative Paul at a table in his prison cell, holding a writing quill by Rembrandt © Everett-Art / shutterstock.com

on the same scene Paul describes in Philippians—continuing to preach the Gospel while imprisoned in Rome (compare Acts 28:30–31 and Philippians 1:12–14). The story of this imprisonment begins at the end of Paul's third missionary journey and lasts for over four years.

Paul's three main missionary journeys are described in Acts 13–14, 15:36–18:22, and 18:23–21:15, respectively. The last of these journeys was a return to the Christian communities in Asia and Greece, and was supposed to end in Jerusalem as Paul's final destination. During one of the last stops on this journey, at Caesarea, a prophet named Agabus foretold that Paul would be arrested in Jerusalem.

Read Acts 21:10–14. What reaction do Paul's companions have to the prophecy of his arrest in Jerusalem? What is Paul's reaction?

_____

_____

As prophesied Paul was seized by a group of Jews shortly after he arrived in Jerusalem. These men falsely accused him of teaching against God's Law and profaning the Temple. They tried to kill Paul, but the Roman tribune intervened and arrested him. When the Jews in Jerusalem continued to plot to murder Paul, he was sent to stand trial before the Roman governor at Caesarea (see Acts 23:12–35). Paul remained in prison in Caesarea for two years before he appealed his case to Caesar and was sent to Rome to present his appeal.

After a long, difficult journey involving storms, shipwreck, and miracles (see Acts 27:1–28:15), Paul arrived in Rome in about A.D. 60. In Rome, Paul was kept under house arrest for two years, and during this time he wrote not only his Letter to the Philippians, but also letters to the Ephesians, the Colossians, and Philemon; these letters from prison are often referred to as

SESSION 2 — PARTNERSHIP IN THE GOSPEL

the "captivity epistles." The New Testament gives no details about St. Paul's final years, but Tradition tells us that he was released after two years of imprisonment in Rome and then arrested again a few years later and martyred around A.D. 64–67 by Emperor Nero.

The Paul writing to the Philippians from house arrest in Rome certainly had come a long way from the Saul who so zealously persecuted and imprisoned the Christians earlier in his life. Compare the accounts of Saul's persecution of Christians in Acts 8:1–3, 9:1–2 and 26:4–11 with Paul's description of his many sufferings for the Gospel in 2 Corinthians 11:23–31. What similarities do you find? How does this fulfill what Jesus says about Paul at the time of his conversion in Acts 9:15–16?

_____

_____

_____

Martyrdom of St. Stephen pediment of the front door of the Saint Etienne du Mont Church, Paris © Zvonimir Atletic / shutterstock.com

The jailer is now the prisoner; and the former persecutor of Christ and his Church now suffers persecution for the Gospel. As a young Pharisee, Saul looked on in approval while Stephen became the first Christian martyr. Now Paul the Apostle waits to discover if he will die the martyr's death as well. But in all this, Paul rejoices because he is able to recognize his sufferings as service to God. What sufferings—great or small—can you offer up today?

_____

Commit – Day 2
Paul's Prison Preaching

Understanding what imprisonment looked like for St. Paul helps to unlock important themes in his Letter to the Philippians.

In the ancient world, prison was not itself a legal penalty. The accused were kept in prison while they waited for their trial, and condemned prisoners were held in prison prior to their execution, but criminals were not sentenced to time in prison as a punishment for their crimes. Also, there was no standard prison experience in Paul's world. As such, his many imprisonments ("far more" than other servants of Christ, according to 2 Corinthians 11:23) differed greatly from each other. Some of these experiences were fairly brutal—such as being confined in stocks after being beaten during his first visit to Philippi in Acts 16:16–40 or his time in the dungeon-like Mamertine prison in Rome immediately before his execution under Emperor Nero. Other imprisonments were comparatively mild, such as his two years of house arrest while awaiting trial before Caesar in Rome (see Acts 28:16–31).

Mamertine prison in Rome, Italy © Vladimir Mucibabic / shutterstock.com

The Roman Empire did not pay to feed its prisoners—if Paul wanted to eat, he had to buy his own food. Thus the financial assistance the Philippians sent to Paul was not just a thoughtful gift to ease the burden of his imprisonment (see Philippians 4:18); it literally helped keep him alive. The Philippians did not forget Paul. They remembered him both in their prayers and in their deeds, providing for his most basic needs. And Paul did not forget their assistance, recounting in his opening prayer that he continually gave thanks to God "in all my remembrance of you."

When has someone recently showed his or her friendship for you? How did this affect your relationship? Who needs your friendship today?

_____

_____

When Paul speaks of his imprisonment in Philippians 1:14, he conveys the stark reality of it by using the Greek word *desmois*, which means "bond" or "fetters," referring to the fact that he spent his entire house arrest chained to a Roman guard to prevent escape. This chain is preserved at the Basilica of St. Paul Outside-the-Walls in Rome, the church built over Paul's tomb. While such house arrest kept Paul out of the horrible conditions of a prison cell, it did limit his freedom.

Tomb of the Apostle Paul and nine chain links. photo © Augustine Institute. All rights reserved.

What seems to be limiting or binding you in your spiritual life? Take some time in prayer today to ask God to use that very thing for his glory.

_____

_____

While limited, Paul still had some freedoms during his house arrest in Rome; he lived in his own rented quarters and could continue to receive visitors and write correspondence (as he does to the Philippians and other Christian communities). Paul ends his Letter to the Philippians with a greeting from "all the saints . . . of Caesar's household" (Philippians 4:22). Even with his limited freedom, Paul's time of imprisonment bears great fruit—a harvest of believers from within the Roman civil service.

Paul speaks of the Gospel becoming known "throughout the whole praetorian guard." The Praetorian Guard was the elite of the Roman military. One of their responsibilities was to keep custody of the accused waiting for trial before Caesar—including St. Paul. Paul's imprisonment, which seems like a calamity of huge proportions, actually gave him access for evangelization that he would not otherwise have had. Paul was a chained prisoner, but the praetorian soldiers who rotated through their service chained to him were Paul's captive audiences. And as Paul received visits from friends, taught, prayed, and wrote his letters, these pagan soldiers heard the Gospel proclaimed and came to faith in Jesus Christ.

As a result, Paul's captivity becomes a means by which the Gospel is spread to the ends of the earth. Paul preaches to Caesar's very household in Rome during his imprisonment, and from Rome the Gospel will travel to every corner of the earth through these new believers—just as Jesus promised it would (see Acts 1:8). Paul is so eager to share with the Philippians the incredible work that God is doing through his imprisonment that it is the first thing he writes about after the letter's opening prayer.

Think of a time God took something in your life that seemed like a failure or setback and used it for good. How did you feel when you were in the middle of that situation? How do you feel about it in hindsight?

_____

_____

"You meant evil against me; but God meant it for good."

—Genesis 50:20

Commit – Day 3
Lectio: Paul's Abandonment to Christ

St. Paul expresses an incredible sense of peace in his Letter to the Philippians. Despite the accusations made against him, his imprisonment, and the envy of his rivals, he maintains his joy and his trust in God. Paul has totally abandoned himself to God's will, and therefore nothing can disturb him. With God's grace, we, too, can surrender so totally to God's divine will that nothing will rob us of his peace.

> **LECTIO:** The practice of praying with Scripture, *lectio divina*, begins with an active and close reading of the Scripture passage. Read the passage below and then answer the questions to take a closer look at some of the details of the passage.

I want you to know, brethren, that what has happened to me has really served to advance the gospel, so that it has become known throughout the whole praetorian guard and to all the rest that my imprisonment is for Christ; and most of the brethren have been made confident in the Lord because of my imprisonment, and are much more bold to speak the word of God without fear.

Some indeed preach Christ from envy and rivalry, but others from good will. The latter do it out of love, knowing that I am put here for the defense of the gospel; the former proclaim Christ out of partisanship, not sincerely but thinking to afflict me in my imprisonment. What then? Only that in every way, whether in pretense or in truth, Christ is proclaimed; and in that I rejoice.

—Philippians 1:12–18

How does Paul refer to those he addresses in this passage?

_____

_____

According to Paul, what has his imprisonment accomplished? What evidence does he offer to support this conclusion?

_____

_____

What are the two different motives Paul sees for others preaching Christ while he is in prison? How does he react to these two different groups of people?

_____

_____

> **MEDITATIO:** *Lectio*, a close reading and rereading of Scripture, is followed by *meditatio*, a time to reflect on the Scripture passage, and to ponder the reason for particular events, descriptions, details, phrases, and even echoes from other Scripture passages that were noticed during *lectio*. Take some time now to mediate on the above verse. To help you get started, consider the following short reflection.

If we understood how to see in each moment some manifestation of the will of God we should find therein also all that our hearts could desire. In fact there could be nothing more reasonable, more perfect, more divine than the will of God. Could any change of time, place, or circumstance alter or increase its infinite value? If you possess the secret of discovering it at every moment and in everything, then you possess all that is most precious, and most worthy to be desired. What is it that you desire, you who aim at perfection? Give yourselves full scope. Your wishes need have no measure, no limit. However much you may desire I can show you how to attain it, even though it be infinite. There is never a moment in which I cannot enable you to obtain all that you can desire. The present is ever filled with infinite treasure, it contains more than you have capacity to hold . . . The will of God is at each moment before us like an immense, inexhaustible ocean that no human heart can fathom; but none can receive from it more than he has capacity to contain, it is necessary to enlarge this capacity by faith, confidence, and love. The early Church clearly understood these instructions and the missionary era began.

—Jean-Pierre de Caussade, *Abandonment to Divine Providence*,
Chapter II, Section III, "How to Discover What Is the Will of God"

How do you think Paul's attitude about the will of God forms his attitude about his imprisonment?

_____

_____

_____

Why do you think Paul is able to rejoice even in the betrayal by his rivals?

_____

_____

_____

> **ORATIO, CONTEMPLATIO, RESOLUTIO:** Having read and meditated on today's Scripture passage, take some time to pray, bringing your thoughts to God (*oratio*) and and to be receptive to God's grace in silence (*contemplatio*). Then end your prayer by making a simple concrete resolution (*resolutio*) to respond to God's prompting of your heart in today's prayer.

Commit—Day 4
Partnership

Handshake © pikcha / shutterstock.com

koinonia/synkoinonia

The Greek word *koinonia* means "partnership." It doesn't refer to a mindset or an attitude but to a real union both in word and deed, as in a business partnership. *Koinonia* means that both parties are fully invested in their joint venture.

As Christians we hear a lot about "fellowship," whether it's in the context of getting to know fellow parishioners over coffee and doughnuts after Mass or developing a deep and intimate sense of community within a Bible study or on a retreat. This fellowship is often referred to as *koinonia*, taking the language from St. Paul's Letter to the Philippians. A deep Christian fellowship is important and necessary in the Christian life. But when Paul speaks of the *koinonia* he shares with the Philippians, he is referring to something on a whole different level, something we should strive for in our own Christian life.

Paul and the Christians in Philippi share something that goes beyond just a sense of community—they are both invested in the work of spreading the Gospel. Paul gives thanks for the Philippians' "partnership in the gospel" (Philippians 1:5). He emphasizes their role as co-workers by calling them *syn-koinonos*, which could be literally translated as "with-partners" (Philippians 1:7). The Philippians are not just partners; they are "with Paul partners."

When Paul uses the word *koinonia* he is evoking the image of partnering together for a business venture. In the business of preaching the Gospel both Paul and the Philippians share the responsibilities, the risks, and the rewards. Whether it is long missionary journeys or long days in prison, the Philippians are "all-in" with Paul in his mission. The *koinonia* between Paul and the Philippians provides an important model for understanding the Church's work of evangelization. The work of preaching the Gospel is not the sole responsibility of either the clergy or the laity—it is the proper work of both.

SESSION 2   PARTNERSHIP IN THE GOSPEL

This intense partnership involves the work of spreading and defending the Gospel and even extends to Paul's own experience of prison (see Philippians 1:7, 4:14). During Paul's imprisonment the Philippians honor their *koinonia* by shouldering some of the financial burden as well as the emotional burden, sending both money and a companion, Epaphroditus. Paul does not view the financial assistance provided by the Philippians as a matter of lay people simply paying for him to go out and do the necessary missionary work—he sees it as a very real participation in that work. Although they perform different roles during his imprisonment, both Paul and the Philippians are involved; both are fully invested. As St. Teresa of Calcutta put it, "Some give by going, others go by giving."

With whom do you partner for the spread of the Gospel? In what ways are you invested in this business venture?

_____

_____

While Paul's work for the Gospel was influencing the Praetorian Guard who attended him, it was not Paul alone who was proclaiming Christ in Rome. Paul notes that "most of the brethren have been made confident in the Lord because of my imprisonment, and are much more bold to speak the word of God without fear" (Philippians 1:14). Not just Paul, but other "brethren" like the Philippians, lay men and women who had come to know Jesus Christ and were baptized into the faith, were boldly sharing the gospel message.

> Finally, the person who has been evangelized goes on to evangelize others. Here lies the test of truth, the touchstone of evangelization: it is unthinkable that a person should accept the Word and give himself to the kingdom without becoming a person who bears witness to it and proclaims it in his turn.
>
> —Pope Paul VI, *Evangelii Nuntiandi*, 24

The *koinonia* shared between Paul and the Philippians is not just something meant for the early Christians. We too should strive for this partnership in the gospel venture, eager and bold to share with others the good work that Christ has begun in our own lives.

The work of spreading the Gospel is not something we are meant to do alone. When Jesus sent his disciples out to announce the kingdom, he sent them out in pairs (see Mark 6:7, Luke 10:1). Paul lives this model for us as he takes various companions with him on his missionary journeys and collaborates with scribes and co-authors in writing his many epistles. Look up the following passages. Who were some of Paul's partners?

Saint Aquila and his wife Saint Priscilla
© Mina Anton / shutterstock.com

SESSION 2 PARTNERSHIP IN THE GOSPEL

Acts 13:1–4 _____

Acts 15:40–16:5 _____

Acts 18:18 _____

Romans 16:22 _____

2 Corinthians 1:1 _____

Philippians 1:1 _____

1 Thessalonians 1:1 _____

In fact, when we see Paul setting out to do something on his own, he doesn't seem to have much success. In Acts 17:16–34 Paul is alone in Athens waiting for Silas and Timothy to join him. The sight of all the idols in the city provokes him, and he starts to argue with just about anyone who will talk to him. He has long discourses with the Greek philosophers in the city, but he wins very few converts compared to his other missionary efforts, undertaken with companions and partners. What does Paul's experience in Athens teach us about the importance of partnership in evangelization?

_____
_____
_____
_____

Like Paul and the Philippians, let us seek out those we can partner with for the sake of the Gospel, doing our part to shoulder the responsibilities and risks and sharing in the rewards.

Commit – Day 5
Truth and Beauty

The Virgin Mary with the Apostles and Other Saints,
Fra Angelico, c. 1423-4, National Gallery, London

The Virgin Mary with the Apostles and Other Saints, Fra Angelico © Restored Traditions. Used by permission.

Fra Angelico was an early Renaissance Italian painter. He combined the life of a devout Dominican friar with that of an accomplished painter. It is said that he would not take up his paintbrush without first saying a prayer. Referred to as "the angelic friar" by his contemporaries, he was beatified by Pope John Paul II in 1982 for his extraordinary personal piety.

Fra Angelico painted *The Virgin Mary with the Apostles and Other Saints* as one of three altarpieces produced for his own friary, San Domenico in Fiesole, before its consecration in 1435. The main large panel of the altarpiece, which still resides at the church but now in a side chapel, shows the Virgin and Child enthroned with angels and Barnabas (the patron saint of the individual that funded the work) and the Dominican saints Thomas Aquinas, Dominic, and Peter Martyr.

Our focus here, however, is not on the main panel but on a portion of the altarpiece's predella. The predella is the painting (or sculpture) along the frame at the bottom of an altarpiece. In later medieval and Renaissance altarpieces, where the main panel consisted of a scene with large static figures, it was common to include a predella below with a number of small-scale narrative paintings (typically three to five scenes in a horizontal format) depicting events from the life of the dedicatee, such as the Life of Christ, or the Life of the Virgin, or a saint.

SESSION 2
PARTNERSHIP IN THE GOSPEL

The Virgin Mary with the Apostles and Other Saints predella consists of five panels. In the central panel the risen and glorified Christ appears in a white robe, holding the flag of the Resurrection, and surrounded by a heavenly host of angels praising and glorifying God in their prayers, song, and musical melodies. The two outer panels on either side show beatified members of the Dominican Order. The inner right panel shows the precursors of Christ (Adam, Moses, John the Baptist, etc.) and the prophets.

The inner left panel, our piece of art for today's reflection, shows Mary in the top right-hand corner (thus in the full predella, she is placed at Jesus's right hand, nearest to her Son and his angelic court). Next to her are three rows of Apostles and evangelists. In the top row, can you make out St. Peter (with his keys), St. Paul (with the sword of his martyrdom), and the young St. John the Evangelist (holding a copy of his Gospel)? Beyond the Apostles and evangelists are Doctors of the Church and members of various religious orders. Can you make out St. Francis (with his tonsured haircut)?

The predella's meticulous execution and decorative detail reflect Fra Angelico's early training as an illuminator of manuscripts. As part of the predella along the bottom frame, this image measured only 12.6" tall by 25.2" wide. In this small space Fra Angelico presents 52 individuals, many holding various objects (books, reed pens, crosiers, staffs, crosses, etc.) and each dressed in their respective robes, tunics, or finely detailed liturgical vestments, beholding the Glorified Christ. (This intricate detail continues in each of the panels, such as the central panel, where the angelic host plays on trumpets, lutes, violins, recorders, tambourines, and even several small pipe organs.) The painting's brilliant color, both in the robes of the multitude of saints and angels, and in its golden background, pictorially exclaims the glory of Heaven, reminding us of St. John's description of the heavenly throne encircled with a rainbow with appearance of jasper, carnelian, and emerald (see Revelation 4:3).

Fra Angelico doesn't portray an anonymous heavenly host, but instead he shows us a myriad of select men and women—precursors, Apostles and saints, many of whom can be clearly identified and named. These are men and women who were partners for the Gospel. Their intimate fellowship with Jesus Christ led to their *syn-koinonia* in sharing the gospel message, and by that partnership they increased the number of souls partaking in this eternal praise of the risen Christ.

In Revelation, St. John describes hearing the sound of trumpets, entering into the heavenly throne room and hearing the winged creatures singing "Holy, Holy, Holy" before the Lord. Look up the following verses. Who does John see and what does he hear in the heavenly throne room?

Revelation 4:10–11 _____

Revelation 5:11–14 _____

And even though St. Paul did not see the heavenly vision that St. John was given, how does Paul describe those who have gone before us?

Hebrews 12:1–2 _____

For the friars who prayed and attended Mass in the church of San Domenico, these predella paintings were a reminder of the partnership and communion they shared, not only with the other friars in the convent, but also with the saints in Heaven. In front of the predella would have stood the tabernacle, its placement a constant reminder that the Lord to whom the heavenly host sings in praise, so wondrously displayed in the predella paintings, is the same glorified Lord that resides in the tabernacle and who was, and is, received at each Eucharist, giving those friars, and us, a taste of the heavenly liturgy we await.

Christ Glorified in Heaven, Fra Angelico © Restored Traditions. Used by permission.

Take a moment to journal your ideas, questions, or insights about this lesson. Write down thoughts you had that may not have been mentioned in the text or the discussion questions. List any personal applications you got from the lessons. What challenged you the most in the teachings? How might you turn what you've learned into specific action?

SESSION 3

FRIENDSHIP IN CHRIST

OPENING PRAYER

Glorious Saint Paul,
Most zealous apostle,
Martyr for the love of Christ,
Give us a deep faith,
A steadfast hope,
A burning love for our Lord,
So that we can proclaim with you,
"It is no longer I who live,
But Christ who lives in me."

Help us to become apostles,
Serving the Church with a pure heart,
Witnesses to her truth and beauty
Amidst the darkness of our days.
With you we praise God our Father:
"To him be the glory, in the Church
And in Christ,
Now and forever."
Amen.

—Prayer to the Apostle St. Paul,
for the Jubilee Year of St. Paul (2008–2009)

INTRODUCTION

Last session, we saw how St. Paul employed the Greco-Roman concept of *koinonia*, business partnership, to model how clergy and laity are called to work together as witnesses of the good news of the Gospel and to build up Christ's Church. In this session, Paul reveals how he is able to joyfully share the Gospel despite his imprisonment. He echoes the Old Testament figure of Job, who also suffered despite his innocence and yet believed in his ultimate vindication. Paul then artfully reworks the Greco-Roman ideals of friendship and citizenship, expanding the Philippians' understanding by calling them to the key virtue of humility, looking first to the interests of others in imitation of Christ. As you watch the video segment, consider how you may imitate the humility of Christ in a deeper way and more perfectly live the Christian ideal of loving God and neighbor.

Connect

Think about your friendships. What do they have in common? Do you have a best friend? What sets this relationship apart from your other friendships?

Do you consider Jesus Christ your friend? If yes, how so? If not, why not? What are some ways you can develop or strengthen your relationship with Jesus Christ?

Video

Watch the video segment. Use the outline below to follow along and take notes.

I. Paul and Job—Philippians 1:19–26
   A. Philippians 1:19 quotes Job 13:16 (Greek Septuagint)
   B. Job giving defense (Job 12–13)
   C. "For I know" (Job 19:25–27)
   D. Job foretold; Jesus accomplished
   E. "For to me to live is Christ, and to die is gain" (Philippians 1:21)

II. Paul's Appeal—Philippians 1:27–2:5
   A. Manner of life ... of your citizenship (*politouthea*)
   B. Christian citizenship is rooted in the Gospel
   C. Paul reworks secular terms for the Gospel
   D. Conflict (*agon*) ... ordeal of a competition
   E. Paul in an ordeal; calls Philippians to have same mind/love

III. Paul on Friendship
   A. Plato—Friendship is being of the same mind
   B. Aristotle—Friendship is *koinonia*; you seek the good of your friend above your own good
   C. Aristotle in *Nicomachean Ethics*—Virtue allows one to live friendship well and find happiness

SESSION 3　　　　　　　　　　　　　　　　　　　　　　　　　FRIENDSHIP IN CHRIST

 D. Humility key to the virtuous life
 E. Humility looks to interest of others before self
 F. Friendship between divinity and humanity impossible for Greeks
 G. Greeks unable to live their ideal of friendship
 H. If we have the mind of Christ, we have ability for friendship with one another, with any social class, even with God

DISCUSS

1. Have you ever encountered any "Jobs" in your life? How did they manage to carry on despite their hardships? What was the source of their strength?

_____

_____

2. According to Dr. Gray, Paul bursts "old wineskins" by reworking the secular notion of citizenship to reflect the Gospel. How does this expansion or reworking expand your understanding of how Christians are called to live as citizens of a heavenly kingdom while still living in this world?

_____

_____

3. Paul shows how the mind of Christ and humility elevate the Greek ideal of friendship. How does this teaching better enable you to live out the command to love God and love your neighbor?

_____

_____

"A virtue is an habitual and firm disposition to do the good. It allows the person not only to perform good acts, but to give the best of himself. The virtuous person tends toward the good with all his sensory and spiritual powers; he pursues the good and chooses it in concrete actions. The goal of the virtuous life is to become like God." —CCC 1803

SESSION 3 — FRIENDSHIP IN CHRIST

MEMORY VERSE

"For to me to live is Christ, and to die is gain."

—Philippians 1:21

CLOSING PRAYER

Lord, make me a channel of thy peace,
that where there is hatred, I may bring love;
that where there is wrong,
I may bring the spirit of forgiveness;
that where there is discord, I may bring harmony;
that where there is error, I may bring truth;
that where there is doubt, I may bring faith;
that where there is despair, I may bring hope;
that where there are shadows, I may bring light;
that where there is sadness, I may bring joy.
Lord, grant that I may seek rather to
comfort than to be comforted;
to understand, than to be understood;
to love, than to be loved.
For it is by self-forgetting that one finds.
It is by forgiving that one is forgiven.
It is by dying that one awakens to Eternal Life.
Amen.

—Prayer of St. Francis

FOR FURTHER READING

Catechism of the Catholic Church, 1785–1786, 1804–1811, 2559, 2796

Commit – Day 1
Job

In Philippians 1:19, Paul expresses joy and confident faith that he will be vindicated and ultimately freed from his chains: "And I shall rejoice. For I know that . . . this will turn out for my deliverance." Paul uses an allusion to Job, an Old Testament example of a righteous man who also remains confident that God will deliver him from his suffering. Many of us are familiar with the ancient story of Job, a wealthy chieftain who suddenly loses his children and property and is stricken with a terrible disease. Job is a man who was "blameless and upright, one who feared God, and turned away from evil" (Job 1:1), yet who suffers loss and pain through no fault of his own. Like Paul, Job suffers great calamity despite being righteous. Yet, despite his affliction and sorrow, Job does not sin by speaking against God (see Job 1:22).

The St. Paul painting in Convento de San Esteban by unknown artist of 17th century © Renata Sedmakova / shutterstock.com

Throughout the Scriptures, we encounter many righteous men and women who display great faith in the face of adversity and suffering. Look up the following three passages. What can we learn from Job and these examples to help us when we face difficulty in our own lives?

1 Samuel 1:1–11, 20 _____

1 Samuel 24:1–12 _____

John 19:25–30 _____

Job is visited by three friends who come to console him. However, instead of consoling him, they begin to assert that his circumstances must be the result of some personal sin of which he must repent. Job reprimands his friends for being unjust toward him when they should display mercy: "Have pity on me, have pity on me, O you my friends, for the hand of God has touched me!" (Job 19:21). Job and his companions enter into a series of debates in which Job decries his wretched state but continually affirms his innocence.

Job and his friends - Drawings by Gustave Dore © Nicku / shutterstock.com

He steadfastly rejects his friends' arguments against him and questions why he has been so afflicted. Cursing the day he was born, Job longs for death as an end to his suffering.

During the debates with his companions, Job becomes increasingly frustrated and calls upon God for an explanation for his suffering. God responds not by justifying his actions, but by reminding Job of God's power and omniscience. God asks Job, "Where were you when I laid the foundation of the earth?" (Job 38:4). In the end, Job repents of his complaints to God, affirming God's power and purpose. God responds by restoring Job's prosperity and family, and blesses Job in his latter days even more than before (see Job 42:12).

> OMNISCIENCE - *having complete or unlimited knowledge, awareness, or understanding; perceiving all things.*

Scripture teaches us that God is trustworthy. What do these verses tell us about God's promises to us?

Jeremiah 29:11 _____

Romans 5:1–5 _____

Romans 8:28 _____

Hebrews 13:5 _____

James 4:8 _____

1 Peter 5:10 _____

Although the story of Job comes to us at least five centuries before Christ, Job gives us an example of perseverance and confident hope that God will ultimately deliver him to eternal life. He exclaims: "For I know that my Redeemer lives, and at last he will stand upon the earth; and after my skin has been thus destroyed, then from my flesh I shall see God" (Job 19:25–26). Likewise, Paul looks toward his future salvation full of hope, convinced of his ultimate vindication because the Redeemer that Job trusted in, Paul knows by name—Jesus Christ.

Let's imitate Job and Paul by closing our reflection today praying the following Act of Hope, trusting in God's great love and his promises, even in the midst of any sufferings and adversity we may face.

O Lord God,
I hope by your grace for the pardon of all my sins
and after life here to gain eternal happiness
because you have promised it
who are infinitely powerful, faithful, kind, and merciful.
In this hope I intend to live and die.
Amen.

Commit—Day 2
Greek Ideal of Friendship

Friendship is one of the most highly valued ideals in the ancient Greek world. For the ancient Greeks, friendship (derived from the Greek word *philia*) described a dispassionate, virtuous love usually between equals. For the Greek classical philosophers like Socrates, Plato, and Aristotle, the Greek city-state or polis is the superior societal structure for helping individuals achieve human flourishing, as the *polis* is a *koinonia* or community built upon friendship. Friends are required to assist each other in the pursuit of living well. Living well requires virtues or excellences. *Philia* relationships provide both the assistance and the means for noble actions in pursuit of a good reputation and fame. Therefore, friendships form the basis for building up the community and making better men.

The School of Athens (Plato and Aristotle surrounded by other Greek philosophers). The fresco of the 16th century in one of the rooms of Raphael (Stanze di Raffaello) in the Vatican Museum © Viacheslav Lopatin/shutterstock.com

In Plato's view, the mutual exchange of services or favors is critical to maintaining genuine *philia* relationships. Genuine friendships can only be sustained among those equal in status and those with similar mindset. Therefore, the wealthy and the poor cannot have a true relationship with each other due to jealousy and ill-will. In his *Laws*, Plato writes, "The ancient pronouncement is true that 'equality produces friendship'" (*Laws*, 757).

In contrast, Aristotle takes friendship to a new height, viewing it as a source of great pleasure and the desire of all men. He distinguishes three types of friendship based on what he sees as the primary characteristics of the objects of love pursued by man: usefulness, pleasantness, and virtuousness or goodness. The lowest form of friendship is one based on utility and is for the sake of self-advantage. The second form of friendship is founded on the pleasure the other provides. The best form of friendship is virtue-friendship and is founded on one's love of the other person's virtue. Virtue-friendship seeks the good of the other. This friendship is based on the goodness of the other and is only possible between the good. Therefore, it is the rarest form of friendship and restricted to the few.

Young boy in wheelchair walking with his friend on the street © Dmytro Gilitukha / shutterstock.com

SESSION 3

FRIENDSHIP IN CHRIST

For the Philippians, who are deeply embedded in Greek culture, this understanding of friendship—the Greek ideal of friendship—is the cultural backdrop from which they read Paul's letter. Aware of this, Paul takes these key concepts and reworks them in light of the Gospel and the Philippians' new citizenship resulting from their Baptism into Christ.

Although friendship is key to the Greek concept of human flourishing, their understanding of friendship remains incomplete. Look up the following verses. How does Christianity elevate and go beyond the Greek understanding of friendship?

John 15:13–15 _____

_____

Galatians 3:27–28 _____

_____

Philemon 1:10–16 _____

_____

While Aristotle's concept of friendship is based on virtue, Dr. Gray explains in the video that a key Christian virtue is missing from the Greek understanding. What is that virtue? Why do you think that virtue is necessary to achieve true friendship?

_____

_____

_____

Paul's particular concern is for the welfare of the church at Philippi. The Church is the Body of Christ and the fellowship or *koinonia* of God's people on earth, so they must learn to live together in love. Paul takes the notion of friendship based on *philia* and elevates it to *agape* by appealing to "their manner of life" and challenging them to live lives "worthy of the gospel of Christ" (Philippians 1:27). How are they to accomplish this? What implication does this have for your own Christian community? What can you do to avoid or heal any divisions in your community?

_____

_____

_____

Commit – Day 3
Lectio: Unity Through the Mind of Christ

St. Paul reminds the Philippians of his own agony and struggles and how he has placed himself in the Lord's hands, confident in his ultimate deliverance. He calls the Philippians to follow his own example, exhorting them to Christian unity in their outlook and manner of living. He reminds them that their citizenship must be rooted in the Gospel of Christ, so that their actions match their preaching and bring honor to Christ. Moreover, this unity of mind, Spirit, and resolve will prepare them to face their opponents and enable them to endure any suffering. As Christians, they too should expect to suffer for Christ. Paul encourages them to stand firm in one Spirit and endure their struggle rooted in the Faith.

> **Lectio:** The practice of praying with Scripture, *lectio divina*, begins with an active and close reading of the Scripture passage. Read the passage below and then answer the questions to take a closer look at some of the details of the passage.

If there is any encouragement in Christ, any incentive of love, any participation in the Spirit, any affection and sympathy, complete my joy by being of the same mind, having the same love, being in full accord and of one mind. Do nothing from selfishness or conceit, but in humility count others better than yourselves. Let each of you look not to your own interests, but also to the interests of others.
—Philippians 2:1–4

Verses 1 and 2 form an if/then conditional statement. Such statements include known factors or hypothetical situations and their consequences. In verse 1, what are the four parts of the "if" conditional clause?

_____
_____
_____

The "then" consequence is that the Philippians are to make Paul's joy complete. What are the four requirements for achieving this consequence?

_____
_____

In the last two verses, how is humility described?

_____
_____

43

SESSION 3

FRIENDSHIP IN CHRIST

> **MEDITATIO:** *Lectio*, a close reading and rereading of Scripture, is followed by *meditatio*, a time to reflect on the Scripture passage, and to ponder the reason for particular events, descriptions, details, phrases, and even echoes from other Scripture passages that were noticed during *lectio*. Take some time now to mediate on the above verse. To help you get started, consider the following short reflection.

Christian spirituality is distinguished by the disciple's commitment to become conformed ever more fully to his Master (cf. Rom 8:29; Phil 3:10,12). The outpouring of the Holy Spirit in Baptism grafts the believer like a branch onto the vine which is Christ (cf. Jn 15:5) and makes him a member of Christ's mystical Body (cf.1 Cor 12:12; Rom 12:5). This initial unity, however, calls for a growing assimilation which will increasingly shape the conduct of the disciple in accordance with the "mind" of Christ: "Have this mind among yourselves, which was in Christ Jesus" (Phil 2:5). In the words of the Apostle, we are called "to put on the Lord Jesus Christ" (cf. Rom 13:14; Gal 3:27).
— John Paul II, Apostolic Letter *Rosarium Virginis Mariae*, 15

Paul rhetorically reminds the Philippians (and us) that his four "ifs" are not hypothetical situations but facts that they have encountered in their conversion to Christ and their incorporation into Christ's Body, the Church, in Baptism. How have you encountered any of these four "ifs" in your own relationship to Jesus Christ?

_____

_____

_____

_____

_____

_____

_____

_____

Jesus Christ. Original oil painting on canvas © Bakhur Nick / shutterstock.com

SESSION 3

FRIENDSHIP IN CHRIST

Having reminded the Philippians of their encounter with Jesus Christ, Paul exhorts them (and us) to manifest this in their lives. In which of the four "thens" do you need to grow? What small, concrete resolution can you make to make progress in this area?

_____

_____

_____

Paul issues a warning against selfishness and conceit. These attitudes are detrimental to the unity to which Christians are called. Take some time to do an examination of conscience using Paul's words:

Have I recently done something from "selfishness or conceit"? _____

_____

Have I counted myself better than others? _____

_____

How have I not looked first to the interests of others? _____

_____

If yes, whom do I need to seek forgiveness from? _____

_____

And what can I do to restore unity and friendship? _____

_____

> **ORATIO, CONTEMPLATIO, RESOLUTIO:** Having read and meditated on today's Scripture passage, take some time to pray, bringing your thoughts to God (*oratio*) and and to be receptive to God's grace in silence (*contemplatio*). Then end your prayer by making a simple concrete resolution (*resolutio*) to respond to God's prompting of your heart in today's prayer.

Commit – Day 4
Humility

The word *humility* evokes lowliness or submissiveness and comes from the Latin *humilitas*, which can be translated "grounded" or "from the earth" as it derives from *humus* (earth). Thus St. Thomas Aquinas quotes St. Isidore describing the humble man (*humo acclinis*) as one "inclined to the lowest place," literally "bent to the ground."

Madonna of Humilty, Fra Angelico © Restored Traditions. Used by permission.

In its teaching on prayer, the *Catechism of the Catholic Church* speaks of humility saying, "But when we pray, do we speak from the height of our pride and will, or 'out of the depths' of a humble and contrite heart (Psalm 130:1)? He who humbles himself will be exalted (cf. Luke 18:9–14); *humility* is the foundation of prayer" (CCC 2559).

In his book *Faith, Hope, Love,* Josef Pieper describes, "Humility is not primarily an attitude that pertains to the relationship of man to man: it is the attitude of man before the face of God. Humility is the knowledge and acceptance of the inexpressible distance between Creator and creature."

Humility allows us to recognize the greatness of God and revere him. Humility encourages one to fear God and keep all his commandments in mind, seeking God's glory in all our thoughts, words, and deeds. Humility is a virtue of self-understanding, which allows us to recognize our own shortcomings and refer all of our sufficiency to God. It is this reverence for God, seeking his will and his ways, that then directs our relationships with our brother and sisters. Humility encourages us to put others before ourselves, for God's sake, because he is also their Creator and Father. As we develop an inward disposition of humility by God's grace, it affects our outward words, deeds, and gestures, restraining us from being in a hurry to speak, being immoderate in our speech, and giving haughty looks; guiding us to outwardly check our laughter and response to others; and redirecting our attention to the needs of others, etc. And our daily effort at putting humility into action, restraining our outward actions, becomes part of the daily offerings we place at the throne of God as we acknowledge him as the author of all good.

St. Augustine sees humility as a foundational virtue, a requirement for a soul to have true virtue as opposed to the mere appearance of virtue. Further, Augustine, writing to his student Dioscorus, encourages him to submit himself to Christ unreservedly, and then describes the way to hold fast to truth, saying, "In that way, the first part is humility; the second, humility; the third, humility: and this I would continue to repeat as often as you might ask direction" (*Letter,* 118). St. Teresa of Calcutta also views humility as the mother of all virtues and the way that our love becomes "real, devoted and ardent. If you are humble nothing will touch you, neither praise nor disgrace, because you know what you are" (as quoted in *The Joy in*

SESSION 3 — FRIENDSHIP IN CHRIST

Loving: A Guide to Daily Living). And St. Francis of Assisi gives us a practical test of our progress in humility: "How much interior patience and humility a servant of God may have cannot be known so long as he is contented. But when the time comes that those who ought to please him go against him, as much patience and humility as he then shows, so much has he and no more" (*Admonition,* 13).

The Prodigal Son by Murillo © Restored Traditions. Used by permission.

Paul exhorts the Philippians to pattern their lives on the supreme example of Jesus Christ, the model of humility. Look up the following verses. How does Jesus describe himself? Or how does the verse show Jesus as the model of humility?

Isaiah 50:6, 53:3–5 _____

Matthew 11:29 _____

Mark 10:45 _____

Luke 22:27 _____

John 6:38 _____

John 15:3–17 _____

2 Corinthians 8:9 _____

Philippians 2:8 _____

These examples from our Lord help us understand Paul's repeated exhortations to "count others better than yourselves" (Philippians 2:3) and through love be servants of one another (Galatians 5:13). These examples from our Lord also shed light on Paul's own actions to exercise humility in imitation of Christ. Paul, who describes humility as placing the needs and interests of others ahead of one's own needs (Philippians 2:4), desires to be with Christ in the heavenly kingdom, but he empties himself of self-interest and places the needs of the Philippians ahead of his own. Even though for Paul "to die is gain" (1:21), he chooses to "remain in the flesh . . . on your account" for the benefit of the church at Philippi (1:24).

Think of examples of people you know who display humility by placing the needs of others ahead of their own. What does that look like?

_____

_____

Below is a beautiful but difficult prayer. Take a moment to earnestly pray the Litany of Humility, asking our Lord and St. Paul to help you grow in humility and to reveal a way that you can serve someone else today.

Litany of Humility

> O Jesus! meek and humble of heart, *Hear me.*
> From the desire of being esteemed, *Deliver me, Jesus.*
> From the desire of being loved, *Deliver me, Jesus.*
> From the desire of being extolled, *Deliver me, Jesus.*
> From the desire of being honored, *Deliver me, Jesus.*
> From the desire of being praised, *Deliver me, Jesus.*
> From the desire of being preferred to others, *Deliver me, Jesus.*
> From the desire of being consulted, *Deliver me, Jesus.*
> From the desire of being approved, *Deliver me, Jesus.*
> From the fear of being humiliated, *Deliver me, Jesus.*
> From the fear of being despised, *Deliver me, Jesus.*
> From the fear of suffering rebukes, *Deliver me, Jesus.*
> From the fear of being calumniated, *Deliver me, Jesus.*
> From the fear of being forgotten, *Deliver me, Jesus.*
> From the fear of being ridiculed, *Deliver me, Jesus.*
> From the fear of being wronged, *Deliver me, Jesus.*
> From the fear of being suspected, *Deliver me, Jesus.*
> That others may be loved more than I, *Jesus, grant me the grace to desire it.*
> That others may be esteemed more than I, *Jesus, grant me the grace to desire it.*
> That, in the opinion of the world,
>   others may increase and I may decrease, *Jesus, grant me the grace to desire it.*
> That others may be chosen and I set aside, *Jesus, grant me the grace to desire it.*
> That others may be praised and I unnoticed, *Jesus, grant me the grace to desire it.*
> That others may be preferred to me in everything, *Jesus, grant me the grace to desire it.*
> That others may become holier than I, provided that I may become as holy as I should,
>   *Jesus, grant me the grace to desire it.*

—Rafael Cardinal Merry del Val (1865–1930)

SUMMIT – DAY 5
TRUTH AND BEAUTY

Madonna of Humility,
Lippo di Dalmasio c. 1390, National Museum, London

Madonna of Humility, Lippo di Dalmasio © Restored Traditions. Used by permission.

Lippo di Dalmasio was a Bolognese artist who painted numerous madonnas, including this *Madonna of Humility*, which is currently held by London's National Gallery.

The Blessed Virgin Mary has been portrayed in Christian art from its earliest days. According to one tradition, Marian iconography follows from a portrait drawn by the Apostle St. Luke. The earliest depictions of Mary date to the second and third centuries and are found in the Roman catacombs. In the early fifth century, the Council of Ephesus reaffirmed the Nicene Christological statements that Jesus was a single divine Person, true God and true man, and that, as a result, the correct title for Mary is that of *Theotokos*, God-bearer. With this reaffirmation, images of Mother and Child increased over the following centuries.

Just as the declarations of the Council of Ephesus influenced Christian art in the centuries following the council, a new image of the Madonna and Child was to appear in the mid-fourteenth century, this time not influenced by a Church council, but rather by the preaching of a new saint and his growing order. At the beginning of the thirteenth century, St. Francis of Assisi began a renewal of Christian devotion and life by his poverty, piety, and preaching. As increasing numbers of men and women renounced the world to follow him, Francis sent out his fellow friars to preach the gospel message not only to the towns of Italy, but to the far reaches of the Christian world.

One of the virtues extolled by Francis was that of humility, which appears numerous times in his writings. Francis saw Holy Humility as a sister of his beloved Lady Poverty. The reason for this emphasis is drawn from the life of Christ, as Francis notes in his Rule: "Let all the brothers strive to follow the humility and poverty of our Lord Jesus Christ." Francis marveled at our Lord's humility, writing:

> Behold daily He humbles Himself as when from His "royal throne" He came into the womb of the Virgin; daily He Himself comes to us with like humility; daily He descends from the bosom of His Father upon the altar in the hands of the priest . . . O humble sublimity! O sublime humility! that the Lord of the universe, God and the Son of God, so humbles Himself that for our salvation He hides Himself under a morsel of bread. Consider, brothers, the humility of God and "pour out your hearts before Him, and be ye humbled that ye may be exalted by Him. Do not therefore keep back anything for yourselves that He may receive you entirely who gives Himself up entirely to you."
>
> —*Admonition,* 1 and *Letter to All the Friars*

Given Francis's love of humility and the widespread preaching of his friars, it is not surprising that a century later the image of the Madonna of Humility begins to appear, first in Italy, and later also in Spain, France, and Germany, as a fruit of Franciscan piety.

While some details change from artist to artist, all depictions show Mary sitting on the ground or a low cushion, a depiction likely drawn from humility's Latin root *humus*, meaning earth or ground. Dalmasio's *Madonna of Humility* is seated on the ground, on a floral bed of red and gold, the depiction of the "low estate of God's handmaiden" (Luke 1:48). She is clothed in a dark robe edged with gold and amber ribbon, picking up the colors of the ground upon with she sits, perhaps a reminder that she too shares the nature drawn from the dust of the earth (Genesis 2:7). But in this earthly frame is a soul completely united to God and who magnifies the Lord (Luke 1:46), a truth perhaps indicated by her interior tunic whose pink color matches that of her Son's garments and those of the heavenly angels above.

As if to remind us of the truth of Jesus's words that "whoever humbles himself will be exalted" (Matthew 23:12), Dalmasio has adorned the humble Virgin with the signs of Revelation 12. Mary wears a crown of twelve stars, with the moon at her feet, and sits before a golden disc clothed with the sun (see Revelation 12:1). The Book of Revelation sets out St. John's vision of the end of the world and the establishment of Christ's kingdom on earth. But this eternal victory begins first in the heart of every believer, who, like Mary, allows humility to bring forth a garden of virtue in his or her life.

What most captures and holds our attention in Dalmasio's image is the gaze between Mother and Child. Even the angels look on in reverent silence as Mary holds Jesus close and their eyes meet. An entire dialogue appears to be taking place as the Mother beholds her Son, and the Lord beholds his most perfect disciple. She, who is pure of heart, sees her God in the infant Child. She, the Lord's most humble disciple who is poor in spirit, experiences here on earth, in the embrace of her Son, the Kingdom of Heaven.

SESSION 3

Take a moment to journal your ideas, questions, or insights about this lesson. Write down thoughts you had that may not have been mentioned in the text or the discussion questions. List any personal applications you got from the lessons. What challenged you the most in the teachings? How might you turn what you've learned into specific action?

SESSION 4

THE MIND OF CHRIST

OPENING PRAYER

Glorious Saint Paul,
Most zealous apostle,
Martyr for the love of Christ,
Give us a deep faith,
A steadfast hope,
A burning love for our Lord,
So that we can proclaim with you,
"It is no longer I who live,
But Christ who lives in me."

Help us to become apostles,
Serving the Church with a pure heart,
Witnesses to her truth and beauty
Amidst the darkness of our days.
With you we praise God our Father:
"To him be the glory, in the Church
And in Christ,
Now and forever."
Amen.

—Prayer to the Apostle St. Paul,
for the Jubilee Year of St. Paul (2008–2009)

INTRODUCTION

When embarking on an important endeavor, it is always helpful to have a guide or model for how to proceed. And what endeavor could be more important than living the right kind of life? After Paul exhorts the Philippians to live out friendship in Christ, he gives them a blueprint for exactly how to do so. St. Paul wants the Philippians to have the mind of Christ, and he paints a beautiful picture of what this means—a life lived out in humble obedience, emptying oneself for others. If we live this life in imitation of Christ, we will also experience the glory of his exaltation by the Father.

Connect

Have you ever felt like you were "of the same mind" with someone else? If so, what enabled this unity? If not, what do you think gets in the way of this unity?

Describe someone who you think provides a good model for the Christian life. What about this person's life do you want to imitate?

Video

Watch the video segment. Use the outline below to follow along and take notes.

I. Same Mind
   A. Having the mindset of Jesus
   B. Mindset/worldview is how you view reality
   C. "Be transformed by the renewal of your mind" (Romans 12:2)
   D. *Metanoia*—word for conversion is transformation of mind

II. Poem/Hymn—Philippians 2:6-11
   A. *Harpagmos*—act of exploiting something for personal gain
   B. Because of Christ's humility (*tapeinoō*), he empties himself (*kenōsis*)
   C. Two parts to poem
      a. Christ makes two descents: (1) "form of God" to man, and (2) man to death
         1. *Isa theou*, "equality with God"—it was illegal for anyone to proclaim themselves *isa theou*
         2. Humility has two key aspects: pouring out of self (*kenōsis*) and obedience

SESSION 4

THE MIND OF CHRIST

    b. God the Father acts to exalt Jesus
       1. Paul declares Jesus is God
         (see Isaiah 45:18–25)
       2. Father's exaltation results in Jesus
         professed as Lord/God
III. How to live Christian life
    A. Jesus is the model/blueprint
    B. "You must be slave (*doulos*) of all"
       (Mark 10:42–22)
    C. Jesus turns the world's idea of authority upside down/right-side up
    D. Giving/serving is how to find happiness
    E. Paul heralds a radical story of a God who became man (when Rome and history are full of men who want to be god)
    F. Road to glory is *kenōsis* and the humility that comes from the mindset of Christ

DISCUSS

1. What was one thing you heard for the first time or that was an "aha" moment for you?

_____

_____

2. What is Paul's "recipe" or plan for making a community of friendship? What are some practical ways to live this out in your own communities (family, parish, school, workplace, etc.)?

_____

_____

3. What does the model of Jesus's life tell us about how to find happiness and fulfillment? What does this look like when we put it into practice?

_____

_____

SESSION 4

THE MIND OF CHRIST

4. Just how radical do you think Paul's preaching of Jesus's *kenosis* was to the pagan Roman citizens of Philippi? How radical is it for us in our own lives? In what areas do we still need to be "transformed by the renewal of [our] minds" to more fully have the mindset of Christ?

_____
_____

MEMORY VERSE

"Have this mind among yourselves, which was in Christ Jesus, who, though he was in the form of God, did not count equality with God a thing to be [exploited], but emptied himself, taking the form of a servant." —Philippians 2:5–7

CLOSING PRAYER

O sweet Name of Jesus,
holy above all names in Heaven and on earth,
and to which every knee, both of men and of angels in Heaven,
on earth and in Hell bends.
You are the way of the just, the glory of the saints,
the hope of those in need, the balm of the sick,
the love of the devout and the consolation of those that suffer.
O, Jesus be to me a help and a protector
so that your Name may be blessed for all times.
Amen.

—A prayer of Thomas à Kempis

FOR FURTHER READING

**Father Mitch Pacwa, *St. Paul on the Power of the Cross* (Our Sunday Visitor, 2008*)*

Commit — Day 1
Metanoia

Do not be conformed to this world but be transformed by the renewal of your mind, that you may prove what is the will of God, what is good and acceptable and perfect. —Romans 12:2

In Philippians 2:5, St. Paul urges the recipients of his letter to "have this mind among yourselves, which was in Christ Jesus." Paul's desire for the Philippians to be united in Christ begins with the transformation of their minds, *metanoia* in Greek. This transformation is the "good work" that God has begun in the Philippians and that Paul prays will be brought to completion (see Philippians 1:6).

It's significant that Paul talks about conversion and being conformed to Christ in terms of *metanoia*, "a transformed mind," and not *metacardia*, "a transformed heart." We learned in the first session that when St. Paul is talking about the mind (*phronein*), he is referring to a mindset or worldview—an entire way of thinking that leads to a way of living. Therefore, if the mind is conformed to Christ, then that person's whole way of looking at the world will be conformed to Christ, who is Truth himself (see John 14:6). *Metanoia* leads to total transformation; and the recognition of and cooperation with Truth will transform every aspect of our self.

How do your choices and actions reflect your own *metanoia* in Christ?

_____

_____

If we understand the transformation of the mind the way Paul originally meant it, then there is no danger of intellectualizing our faith and ignoring the need to put our faith into practice in our daily lives. We are not just seeking knowledge about God; rather we are seeking knowledge of him—to know him, to love him, and to love like him. As we strive to take on the mindset of Christ, the complete transformation of *metanoia* becomes apparent in our actions. As we begin to think like Christ, then we will begin to act like Christ.

Of course, our minds are not simply blank slates just waiting to be conformed to the mind of Christ. In his Letter to the Romans, St. Paul warns us to be wary of an alternative. The world is constantly vying for our attention and allegiance, and if we are not careful we will be conformed to this world, rather than to Christ and our heavenly homeland.

Thinking © ESB Professional / shutterstock.com

SESSION 4 — THE MIND OF CHRIST

What are some ways that the world is beckoning you to be conformed to it instead of to Christ? How are you combatting the call of the world?

_____

_____

> *Finally, brethren, whatever is true, whatever is honorable, whatever is just, whatever is pure, whatever is lovely, whatever is gracious, if there is any excellence, if there is anything worthy of praise, think about these things.*
> —Philippians 4:8

Reading the Gospels and the lives of the saints daily helps us to "think about these things." The more familiar we are with the life of Jesus and holy men and women, the easier it will be to imitate their actions in our own lives.

Another important part of being transformed by the renewal of our minds is our responsibility to form our consciences. The *Catechism of the Catholic Church* calls the conscience and "a judgment of reason whereby the human person recognizes the moral quality" of an act (CCC 1778). It also says that we are all under an obligation to obey our conscience and to "follow faithfully what [we know] to be just and right" (CCC 1778). But a person is not born preprogrammed to correctly judge right and wrong. Each of us must form our consciences in accordance with God's truth: "Conscience must be informed and moral judgment enlightened," as the *Catechism* says (CCC 1783). This process of formation takes an entire lifetime, and doing it correctly is crucial to having the mind of Christ. A conscience that is rightly formed protects us from conformity to this world and puts us on track for sharing the mind of Christ. Scripture, the *Catechism* and other writings of the Church, the writings of the saints, the examples and guidance of faithful people—these all help us to form our consciences.

Ask the Holy Spirit for guidance and grace, and pick one concrete action you can make this week to continue in the process of the renewal of your mind.

_____

_____

_____

Commit – Day 2
The Mind of Christ

St. Paul's Letter to the Philippians is full of encouragement and exhortations to live a holy Christian life. Paul lives out an incredible example of these ideals in his own life (see 1 Corinthians 11:1), and he seems confident that the Philippians, by the grace of God, can do so as well. We have the same calling, but we often encounter a vast distance between the description of the Christian life we find in the New Testament and the actual experience of trying to live it out. It's one thing to resolve to "have this mind among yourselves, which was in Christ Jesus" (Philippians 2:5) and quite another to remember and act upon that resolution when a family member or co-worker or fellow parishioner gets on our nerves or wrongs us.

Paul doesn't leave us to figure out the perfect Christian life on our own. He doesn't even leave us with only the general instruction to have the mind of Christ. Paul sees himself as a master architect, building up the people of God into a holy temple. And just as a good architect lays out his project carefully and in detail, Paul gives us a clear blueprint for how to live a life in imitation of Christ. At the heart of his Letter to the Philippians is an exquisite hymn to Jesus Christ—the source and model of the Christian life—which shows us how to be conformed to the mind of Christ.

Rolls of architecture blueprints © Gargantiopa / shutterstock.com

> *"According to the commission of God given to me, like a skilled master builder I laid a foundation, and another man is building upon it. Let each man take care how he builds upon it. For no other foundation can any one lay than that which is laid, which is Jesus Christ."* —1 Corinthians 3:10–11

The great hymn in Philippians 2:6–11 can be divided into two parts: Jesus's action of humbling himself, and the Father's action of exalting his Son. If—and only if—we imitate Christ in his obedient humility, we will also share in his exaltation and glory.

First comes the downward motion of Christ humbling himself. In Philippians 2:6, Paul says that Christ Jesus, "though he was in the form of God, did not count equality with God a thing to *harpagmos*." The Greek word *harpagmos* refers to the act of exploiting something for personal benefit. A common example in the first century Roman world would have been a government official who exploited his position and privilege for his own gain, rather than using that position to serve the people. Being familiar with this secular grasping at privilege and status in order to exalt oneself, the Philippians' would have been shocked to hear Paul describe that Jesus does the exact opposite. In a single sentence Paul declares not only that Jesus is God, but that he is a God who willingly sets aside the glory of his divinity for the sake of man. He does this in order to restore the likeness of God in man, that man may participate in divine life.

Because of sin God seemed distant to man. In order to restore the relationship that was lost through sin, God took "the form of a [slave]" (Philippians 2:7), and became man. Jesus Christ, the second Person of the Blessed Trinity, assumed human nature without leaving his transcendences or divinity. The word that Paul uses to describe Jesus's downward movement of taking on a human nature is *kenōsis*, a Greek word that means to "empty out." As Paul puts it in another place, "Though he was rich, yet for your sake he became poor, so that by his poverty you might become rich" (2 Corinthians 8:9). Jesus is God, but he is a God who empties himself to reach us.

Serbian Icon of the Kingship of Christ. Artwork by J. Vasilievic / Restored Traditions. Used by permission.

After the descent comes the upward motion of the Father exalting Jesus, the second part of the poem. As Paul proclaims: "Therefore God has highly exalted him" (Philippians 2:9). It is precisely Jesus's humility and obedience that lead to his exaltation. It goes against every social norm—not only of the first century, but also of today—to expect exaltation to come as a result of radical humility. Yet this is the clear model for the Christian life, lived out by Jesus and presented not only by Paul in this hymn, but also by other Apostles (see James 4:10, and 1 Peter 5:6). If we want to have the mind of Christ and live a holy Christian life, we too must empty ourselves. Having read the blueprint, we must also lay down our lives and let ourselves be built upon the perfect foundation of Christ, building not with wood, hay, or straw, but with the gold, silver, and precious stones of humble obedience.

Read Philippians 2:3–4. How does Paul urge us to live out the uniquely Christian virtue of humility? (Remember, in verse 4 there is no "only" in the original Greek!) What are two or three things you can do this week to practice this humility?

_____

_____

The key to humility is obedience. Jesus emptied himself and was "obedient unto death" (Philippians 2:8). Take some time in prayer to reflect on whether you have been obedient to God and to those he has put over you, and how you can perfect your obedience.

_____

_____

Commit – Day 3
Lectio: Slaves of All

As we have seen, the willingness to place oneself at the service of others is an important theme in St. Paul's Letter to the Philippians. Paul identifies himself and Timothy as servants or slaves (*douloi*) of Jesus Christ (see Philippians 1:1), and in his great hymn to Christ he says that Jesus took "the form of a servant (*doulos*)" when he emptied himself in obedience to the Father's will (Philippians 2:7). Our call to service is to be lived out in imitation of our Lord, who came not to be served but to serve. Jesus's words to his Apostles in Mark 10:35–45 help us understand how we are to humble ourselves in service along with Christ.

> **LECTIO:** The practice of praying with Scripture, *lectio divina*, begins with an active and close reading of the Scripture passage. Read the passage below and then answer the questions to take a closer look at some of the details of the passage.

And James and John, the sons of Zebedee, came forward to him, and said to him, "Teacher, we want you to do for us whatever we ask of you." And he said to them, "What do you want me to do for you?" And they said to him, "Grant us to sit, one at your right hand and one at your left, in your glory." But Jesus said to them, "You do not know what you are asking. Are you able to drink the chalice that I drink, or to be baptized with the baptism with which I am baptized?" And they said to him, "We are able." And Jesus said to them, "The chalice that I drink you will drink; and with the baptism with which I am baptized, you will be baptized; but to sit at my right hand or at my left is not mine to grant, but it is for those for whom it has been prepared." And when the ten heard it, they began to be indignant at James and John. And Jesus called them to him and said to them, "You know that those who are supposed to rule over the Gentiles lord it over them, and their great men exercise authority over them. But it shall not be so among you; but whoever would be great among you must be your servant, and whoever would be first among you must be slave of all. For the Son of man also came not to be served but to serve, and to give his life as a ransom for many."

—Mark 10:35–45

Who is asking the question of Jesus? What is their request?

_____

_____

How do the other Apostles react to this question?

_____

_____

How many times does Jesus use a form of "serve" or "slave" in his response?

_____

SESSION 4

THE MIND OF CHRIST

> **MEDITATIO**: *Lectio*, a close reading and rereading of Scripture, is followed by *meditatio*, a time to reflect on the Scripture passage, and to ponder the reason for particular events, descriptions, details, phrases, and even echoes from other Scripture passages that were noticed during *lectio*. Take some time now to mediate on the above verse. To help you get started, consider the following short reflection.

Service in the Gospel, unlike service in the world, is not the proper characteristic of the inferior, of the one in need, but rather of the superior, of the one who is raised high. Jesus says that, in His Church, it is first of all "the leader" who must be "like the one who serves" (Luke 22:26), the first must be "slave to all" (Mark 10:44). . . . In John Paul II's book "Gift and Mystery," he expresses this meaning of authority in the Church with a strong image, in the form of a few verses he composed while in Rome at the time of the Council: "It is you, Peter. Here you wish to be the Ground / On which the others walk ... so they can reach the place / Whither you guide their steps / As the rock bears the hoof-marks of the flock."

We finish by listening to the words spoken by Jesus to his disciples immediately after he had washed their feet, as though he were speaking to us, here and now: "Do you understand what I have done to you? You call me Master and Lord, and rightly, so I am. If I, then, the Lord and Master, have washed your feet, you must wash each other's feet. I have given you an example, so that you may copy what I have done to you" (John 13:12–15).

—"Love Must Be Active: The Social Relevance of the Gospel,"
Fourth Lenten homily from Father Raniero Cantalamessa to Benedict XVI
and the Roman Curia, April 8th, 2011

What motivates James and John to make their request of Jesus? How does Jesus redirect their focus?

_____

_____

_____

What is the worldly model of leadership? What model does Jesus offer in contrast?

_____

_____

_____

SESSION 4

THE MIND OF CHRIST

What does it mean to be "slave of all"?

_____

_____

_____

> **ORATIO, CONTEMPLATIO, RESOLUTIO:** Having read and meditated on today's Scripture passage, take some time to pray, bringing your thoughts to God (*oratio*) and and to be receptive to God's grace God in silence (*contemplatio*). Then end your prayer by making a simple concrete resolution (*resolutio*) to respond to God's prompting of your heart in today's prayer.

_____

_____

_____

_____

_____

_____

Commit – Day 4
Equality with God

Jesus Christ enthroned and surrounded by angels © mountainpix / shutterstock.com

In his great hymn to Christ in Philippians 2:6–11, St. Paul talks about Jesus being "in the form of God," having "equality with God," and having a "name which is above every name," which will lead all of creation to "confess that Jesus Christ is Lord." Read against a Christian background, these words seem familiar and perhaps even anticlimactic—of course Jesus is Lord, equal to God, and deserving of our worship. But in the first century, this foundational belief in the divinity of Christ was something radical and counter-cultural. The words of Philippians 2:6–11 reverberated like shock waves, crashing through religious, cultural, and even legal norms of the first-century world.

The Jews were defined by their strict monotheism, and the Greeks and Romans believed in gods who were proud and powerful. For both Jew and pagan, the idea of this God-man who suffered and died was strange and scandalous. To affirm this central and unique doctrine of Christianity, Paul proclaims the divinity of Christ in no uncertain terms—first by using and subverting language familiar to Greco-Roman culture, and then by also echoing prophetic language of the Hebrew Scriptures.

In Philippians 2:6, Paul says that Jesus was "in the form of God" (*morphae theou*). The phrase "in the form of God" in modern English might sound like Jesus just resembled God in some way—perhaps a mere man simply representing God. But the phrase *morphae theou* in verse 6 indicates the true divinity of Christ, just as the phrase *morphae doulou* in verse 7 asserts the full humanity of Christ ("taking the form of a servant (*morphae doulou*), being born in the likeness of men"). In fact, the *Catechism* refers to this passage from Philippians as a hymn in which "the Church sings the mystery of the Incarnation" (CCC 461), the mystery of God becoming man.

In verse 6, Paul also states that Jesus "did not count equality with God (*isa theou*) a thing be grasped." Paul's use of *isa theou* is intentional—*isa theou* was an important Greek title meaning "to be like the gods" or "to be divine." In the ancient Greco-Roman world, this title was the highest honor that could be bestowed on a person. Alexander the Great took this title for himself, as did

Caesar Augustus. In fact, after Augustus had the Roman Senate declare his father Julius to be divine, he then started calling himself "son of god." Augustus became so jealous of this divine title that he declared the use of *isa theou* to be reserved only for the Roman emperors and their households. Paul's application of the title to Christ is not only bold, but illegal!

As Paul continues his hymn, he makes it very clear that the Father's exaltation of Christ is the highest, most perfect exaltation possible: "[God has] bestowed on him the name which is above every name, that at the name of Jesus every knee should bow, in heaven and on earth and under the earth, and every tongue confess that Jesus Christ is Lord, to the glory of God the Father" (Philippians 2:9–11).

Alexander the Great © Haris vythoulkas / shutterstock.com

Paul is a gifted author, but these are not his own words. He's drawing on imagery out of an important passage from the prophet Isaiah. In the eighth century B.C., the people of Judah had fallen into idolatry. Isaiah called them back to a faithful relationship with the one true God, giving assurance that God would keep his promises to his faithful but also prophesying just punishment for those who refused to turn away from their false gods.

Isaiah 45 is one of the strongest treatises against idolatry in the entire Old Testament. Read Isaiah 45:18–25 and Philippians 2:9–11. What echoes of Isaiah do you find in Philippians? What is Paul saying about Jesus when he makes these references to Isaiah 45?

_____

_____

In a few short verses, Paul makes it clear to both Jews and Greeks that Jesus is God, and at the same time shows that it is humility that brings the exaltation of Christ the eternal Lord and King.

Read Philippians 2:9–11 again. What can you do this week to make a point of acknowledging that Jesus is Lord?

_____

_____

"The title *Pantocrator* is the Greek translation used for two Hebrew titles for God: YHWH Sabaoth, "Lord of Hosts," and *El Shaddai*, "God Almighty." This traditional title for Christ indicates his divinity"

Christ Pantocrator fresco inside Monreale cathedral © Banet / shutterstock.com

Commit – Day 5
Truth and Beauty

The Crucifixion,
Bartolomé Esteban Murillo, ca. 1675, The Metropolitan Museum of Art, New York

Jesus Christ on the Cross by Murillo © Restored Traditions. Used by permission.

Bartolomé Esteban Murillo (1617–1682) was the last great painter of the Spanish Golden Age. Murillo grew up in Seville, in the Andalusia region of southern Spain, and was initially influenced by the great Spanish artists Ribera and Zurbarán (who some considered the Spanish Caravaggio for his masterful use of chiaroscuro—the contrasting of light and shade). During a trip to Madrid in 1658, Murillo had the chance to encounter paintings by Rubens and Italian Renaissance artists, which further influenced his style. The combination of these influences on Murillo's work made him a much loved and leading painter of Seville.

After reaching its zenith in the sixteenth century, the Seville that Murillo grew up in went through enormous turmoil and suffering in the seventeenth century. In 1649, the plague swept through the city and reduced its population nearly by half. This was followed only two years later by famine and crop failure. And the silting of the city's main river pushed trade south to Cádiz. Murillo saw the suffering of others around him and experienced it in his own life, living through the death not only of his wife, but also five of their nine children. Such suffering could have led Murillo to portray only despair in his work, but with his Baroque realism and masterful use of light and shadow, Murillo painted images that allowed his viewer to experience supernatural hope in the midst of simplicity, want, and suffering.

While Murillo did several crucifixion scenes, the image of our reflection today is a small painting (only 20 by 13 inches) done in the last decade of his life, that today resides in New York's Metropolitan Museum of Art and is related to a much larger crucifixion painting (72 by 43 inches) that resides in Madrid's Prado Museum. This small crucifixion scene is a wonderful example of Counter-Reformation art, its sole focus on Christ and the gospel scene of the crucifixion, without the distractions of unnecessary details.

In his Gospel, St. John recounts that after "Jesus had received the vinegar, he said, 'It is finished'; and he bowed his head and gave up his spirit" (John 19:30). The soldiers are hurried by the Jews to finish things up so that the bodies can be taken down ahead of the approaching Sabbath. In response, the soldiers break the legs of the thieves on either side of Jesus, but seeing that Jesus had already expired they instead pierce his side with a lance. It is at this point in the crucifixion events that Murillo allows us to stand at the foot of the cross. We can put ourselves into the scene, imagining ourselves standing next to the Apostle John, he "who saw it [and] has borne witness," as he recalls the prophecy, "They shall look on him whom they have pierced" (John 19:37).

The other three gospel writers each recount that "there was darkness over the whole land" for the three hours Jesus hung on the Cross (see for example, Mark 15:33). We are immersed in that darkness in Murillo's painting. His strong brush strokes allow us to feel the oppressive heaviness of the black clouds around us. In the midst of this darkness, the primary source of light in the painting is not natural, but the supernatural light emanating from the body of the Son of God, allowing us to count his ribs, to see the stretched muscles in his arms as they bear the full weight of his now limp body.

Against his luminous body we can make out the blood draining from the wounds in his hands and feet, and from his pierced side. He is so close; there are no crowds or soldiers or even the two thieves to obstruct our view. We appear to be mere inches from our Savior. We are almost drawn to reach into the picture and wrap our arms around the foot of the Cross and join our tears to the suffering our Lord has endured for our sake. As we reach for the foot of the Cross we see the last light of day as the sun sets on the horizon beyond the city of Jerusalem, which is barely visible in the shadows. The Son of God has breathed his last, as the sun gives up its last rays. And yet, this glow on the horizon also gives us hope, a reminder that in three days the sun will break over the horizon, bringing the dawn of a new age with the Resurrection of the Son of God and the hope that we too might rise with him at the end of our lives and join him where "neither shall there be mourning nor crying nor pain any more, for the former things have passed away" (Revelation 21:4).

St. Ignatius of Loyola, a Spanish saint who lived in the previous century before Murillo, encouraged Christians in contemplating Scripture to use their senses in an imaginative way to make a gospel passag real and alive, so as to engage with the Word of God himself. Murillo's painting jump-starts us into just such an encounter. As you finish this time of reflection, use Murillo's painting to enter more fully into this gospel scene, looking on him who suffered out of love for you. Like the centurion, may you be filled with awe, and say, "Truly this was the Son of God!" (Matthew 27:54).

Take a moment to journal your ideas, questions, or insights about this lesson. Write down thoughts you had that may not have been mentioned in the text or the discussion questions. List any personal applications you got from the lessons. What challenged you the most in the teachings? How might you turn what you've learned into specific action?

SESSION 5

IMITATIO CHRISTI

OPENING PRAYER

Glorious Saint Paul,
Most zealous apostle,
Martyr for the love of Christ,
Give us a deep faith,
A steadfast hope,
A burning love for our Lord,
So that we can proclaim with you,
"It is no longer I who live,
But Christ who lives in me."

Help us to become apostles,
Serving the Church with a pure heart,
Witnesses to her truth and beauty
Amidst the darkness of our days.
With you we praise God our Father:
"To him be the glory, in the Church
And in Christ,
Now and forever."
Amen.

—Prayer to the Apostle St. Paul,
for the Jubilee Year of St. Paul (2008–2009)

INTRODUCTION

In both the Old and New Testaments, God calls his people to become more like him. At Mount Sinai, the Israelites received the charge: "You shall be holy; for I the Lord your God am holy" (Leviticus 19:2). During the Sermon on the Mount, Jesus reiterated this command: "You, therefore, must be perfect, as your heavenly Father is perfect" (Matthew 5:48). In his Letter to the Philippians, Paul paints a vivid picture of how to pursue this goal. We are not called to strive after holiness in some abstract way, but to do so by imitating Christ—specifically in his sacrificial gift of self. It is a call to pour ourselves out as an offering to God, just as Jesus did on the Cross. Embracing this "loss of all things," Paul tells us, is the only way to "gain Christ and be found in him" (Philippians 3:8–9).

The mocked Jesus wearing a crown of thorns and a scarlet cloak, holding a reed by C. Bloch © Restored Traditions. Used by permission.

Connect

What is one task or project you have that is never quite finished and always requires more work?

Share about a time you gave up something that was good in order to get something that was even better.

Video

Watch the video segment. Use the outline below to follow along and take notes.

I. Philippians 2:12–18—Application of Poem
   A. We work not to obtain salvation, but to remain justified and not lose citizenship
   B. Good works are God's grace active in us
   C. "Blameless . . . without blemish" is language for lamb to be fit sacrifice
   D. "Shine as lights"
      a. Isaiah 49:6—Suffering Servant to be a light to the nations
      b. Isaiah 49:4—Servant laments, "I have labored in vain," but Paul has not labored in vain
   E. Philippians' faith will require sacrifice, which leads to a *kenosis*
   F. Paul's sacrifice
      a. Libation is drink offering poured
         1. atop some sacrificial offerings and
         2. at the base of the altar for daily *tamid* offering
      b. Paul is being poured out in chains in prison

II. Philippians 2:19–30—Models of Jesus
   A. Sends Timothy (letter and in person; Scripture and Tradition)
   B. Sends Epaphroditus (for his welfare and that of the Philippians)
   C. Paul shows Timothy and Epaphroditus as models of Jesus

SESSION 5　　　　　　　　　　　　　　　　　　　　IMITATIO CHRISTI

III. Philippians 3:1–16—Loss and Gain
   A. "Look out for the dogs"—reversing language
      Jews used for Gentiles
   B. Business accounting language
     a. Paul lost many worldly goods
     b. "*Koinonia* in his suffering" evokes language
       of hymn
   C. Paul shows his life as an *imitatio Christi*
     a. Not preaching for gain, but pours himself
       out for the mission
     b. Paul suffered so as to be conformed to Christ
   D. "I press on" (3:12)—race metaphor

DISCUSS

1. What was one thing you heard for the first time or that was an "aha" moment for you?

_____
_____

2. What does Paul urge the Philippians to do in order to "shine as lights in the world" (Philippians 2:14–16)? What are some practical things that we can do to live out this same calling in our own lives?

_____
_____

3. How does Paul show Timothy and Epaphroditus to be models of Jesus? Is there someone in your life who models Jesus in this way? Is there someone to whom you model Jesus in this way?

_____
_____

SESSION 5 — IMITATIO CHRISTI

MEMORY VERSE

"But whatever gain I had, I counted as loss for the sake of Christ. Indeed I count everything as loss because of the surpassing worth of knowing Christ Jesus my Lord." —Philippians 3:7–8

CLOSING PRAYER

O most holy Jesus,
you humbled yourself in obedience.
Teach me to embrace the Cross and bear the sufferings of my life
with patience and humility.
Give me the grace and the strength to do all things
without grumbling or questioning,
to be blameless and innocent and without blemish,
and to shine as a light in the world.
May my life and my faith
be an acceptable sacrificial offering in your sight.
I place my trust in you as the source of all my joy and consolation—
do with me as you please.
Amen.

FOR FURTHER READING

Scott Hahn. *A Pocket Guide to St. Paul* (Our Sunday Visitor: 2008)

Commit—Day 1
Blameless and Without Blemish

Animal sacrifice is one of the most striking aspects of the Hebrew religion. Whole sections of Leviticus and Deuteronomy are devoted to the laws governing what to sacrifice, and when and how to do it (and whole sections of the prophets warn Israel of the impending judgment for failing to observe these laws). With all of the rules, regulations, blood, and fire, the Old Testament sacrificial system can easily appear quite disconnected from Christianity. The Old Covenant way to worship God was to offer sacrifices. The New Covenant way is to worship "in spirit and truth" (John 4:23), so no more sacrifice necessary, right?

Innocent © Erce / shutterstock.com

While bloody animal sacrifice (which was a temporary condescension of God after the golden calf) is clearly ended, St. Paul understands that sacrifice still has its place in the New Covenant worship. After Paul lays out the self-sacrificial model of Christ's descent in humility and his exaltation to glory in Philippians 2:6–11, he urges the Philippians to continue to live in obedience and faithfulness "that you may be blameless and innocent, children of God without blemish" (2:15). Here Paul uses the language of the Old Testament sacrificial laws, which required that an offering for sacrifice be without blemish.

> *"You shall not sacrifice to the LORD your God an ox or a sheep in which is a blemish, any defect whatever; for that is an abomination to the LORD your God."*
> —Deuteronomy 17:1

The Philippians are to be blameless and innocent—they themselves are now to be a sacrifice. Paul reminds the Philippians that the same purity is required of the offering of their own selves, and he encourages them to live lives that are worthy of being offered as a sacrifice to God.

It's interesting that Paul uses such intense Temple language in a letter written to a church made up largely of Gentiles (remember, Paul's first converts in Philippi were Gentile God-fearers—there wasn't even a Jewish synagogue in the city). Paul draws on the liturgical traditions of the Jews to make a striking point about sacrifice, but this concept goes even further back than the laws given to the Israelites at Mount Sinai.

The understanding that worshipping God necessarily involves some kind of sacrifice is as old as creation—a command inscribed on human nature itself. When God created the first man, he placed him in the garden to till it and "keep it" (Genesis 2:15). The same Hebrew verb is used to describe the liturgical responsibilities of the priests and Levites who are to "keep charge" of the tabernacle (see Numbers 1:53; 1 Chronicles 23:32; Ezekiel 44:14). God's first command to Adam concerned priestly duties, and the quintessential duty of the priest is to offer sacrifice.

Even after the Fall and exile from paradise, we see the next generation carrying on these priestly duties when Cain and Abel bring their sacrifices to God in Genesis 4. Mankind was created to worship God and to worship through offering sacrifice. The story of Cain and Abel's two offerings reveals something crucial about this sacrificial system built into human nature. Read Genesis 4:3–7. What are the differences between the brothers' offerings? Why does God accept one and not the other?

Cain and Abel by Ghiberti. © Timur Kulgarin / shutterstock.com

_____

_____

On the surface it may seem like God just likes sheep better than vegetables. But verse 5 indicates that it wasn't so much a problem with "what" was offered but with the heart of the one offering. Cain's sacrifice is unacceptable because of the spirit in which he offers it. The external offering is meant to be a visible sign of the internal disposition. The primary offering is to be of the heart—a pure heart. Read Psalm 51:10, 17. What does David's prayer reveal about the relationship between inner disposition and an acceptable act of worship?

_____

_____

It's easy to offer the blemished calf, to make a half-hearted sacrifice, to grumble and question (see Philippians 2:14); such an offering does not cost us much. We are called to be willing to sacrifice like David, who said, "I will not offer burnt offerings to the Lord my God which cost me nothing" (2 Samuel 24:24). The unblemished sacrifice is costly, and, by necessity, it can only proceed from a heart overflowing with love. St. Paul exhorts the Philippians to have an unblemished and pure heart, from which they will be able to offer an acceptable sacrifice of obedience, faithfulness, and good works.

Spend some time in prayer considering the sacrifices you offer to God and the spirit in which you offer them. Ask God to help you recognize areas that need improvement.

_____

_____

Commit—Day 2
Koinonia in Christ's Suffering

We have seen how St. Paul's Letter to the Philippians draws on the liturgical traditions of Israel regarding sacrifice. But this begs the question: Why? If Jesus established a new covenant, why is Paul still using the language and imagery of the old?

If we look at the Old and New Testaments as telling the story of two completely different religions—as many people tend to do—it makes no sense. But Paul recognizes the continuity between the old and new and that they are two parts of one story. Paul understands that Jesus is the bridge between the sacrificial system of the Old Testament and the worship "in spirit and in truth" of the New. As Jesus himself says, he came "not to abolish [the law and the prophets] but to fulfill them" (Matthew 5:17). Regarding that fulfillment, Jesus doesn't overturn the Old Testament precedent of sacrifice—he transforms it. In place of the series of animal sacrifices which must be repeated over and over, Jesus offers his once for all, efficacious sacrifice on the Cross.

Agnus dei © ananas / shutterstock.com

But Christ's sacrifice doesn't preclude the need for us to offer our own sacrifice. Quite the opposite. We are invited—actually required—to participate in Christ's sacrifice. Look up the following verses. What are we called to as disciples of Christ?

Colossians 1:24 _____

_____

2 Timothy 2:3 _____

_____

2 Peter 2:21 _____

_____

Jesus's sacrifice on the Cross was absolutely perfect and complete. Through faith and Baptism we receive a share in Jesus Christ's priestly vocation (see CCC 784), and if we are going to follow and be found "in Christ," we must imitate and live Jesus's self-sacrifice in our own lives. In Philippians 3:1–11, Paul gives a brief summary of what he has sacrificed in order to follow Christ. Paul uses technical business language (similar to the language he used to talk about his partnership with the Philippians) to describe the exchange by which he suffers the "loss" of all things and

Saint Peter and Saint Paul in Mamertine Prison © Sergey Kohl / shutterstock.com

"gains" Christ. According to Paul, nothing that he had before Christ profited him. But when he sacrifices all that he has, he more than breaks even—he gains Christ, and that is everything.

What have you been called to give up in order to gain Christ? What do you feel you have gained in return?

_____

_____

Christian martyrs in the coliseum by J. Gerome. © Restored Traditions. Used by permission.

This business language of gains and losses emphasizes the surpassing worth of being in Christ Jesus and how worthless anything else is by comparison. But it's not just a matter of giving up a few worldly goods here and there. Paul says in verse 10 that this righteousness that comes through faith means he shares in Christ's sufferings. Paul uses the word *koinonia* again to describe this participation. It's not a matter of Jesus suffering and Paul reaping the benefits—it's a partnership. The only way to have a share in the Resurrection is to also share in Christ's suffering and Death. It's the same point that Paul has made several times already in his letter—to conform oneself to Christ means to be conformed to the Cross.

The "Little Way" of St. Thérèse of Lisieux exemplifies the call to a cruciform life. "Miss no single opportunity of making some small sacrifice, here by a smiling look, there by a kindly word; always doing the smallest right and doing it all for love." Thérèse offered everything to God with love—no matter how small or mundane the suffering. This habit of looking upon every sacrifice as a chance to draw close to our crucified Lord enabled her to face sickness and suffering with such peace, and even joy, that she was able to say on her deathbed, "I have reached the point of not being able to suffer any more, because all suffering is sweet to me."

No sacrifice is too small or ordinary to draw us closer to Christ, and it is these daily offerings made over and over again that allow faith to grow and blossom into the courage of the martyr. What daily sufferings or sacrifices can you embrace and unite to the suffering of Christ in *koinonia*?

_____

_____

Commit – Day 3
Lectio: The Suffering Servant

As the long-awaited Messiah, Jesus fulfills not only the glorious Old Testament prophecies of restoration and redemption, but also prophecies of sacrifice and suffering—including Isaiah's prophecy of the Suffering Servant of the Lord. St. Paul's Letter to the Philippians makes it clear that while he understands Isaiah's Suffering Servant to be fulfilled first and foremost in Christ, Paul sees a fulfillment in himself and in each member of Christ's Body who shares in the sufferings of Christ and becomes "like him in his death" (Philippians 3:10).

> **LECTIO:** The practice of praying with Scripture, *lectio divina*, begins with an active and close reading of the Scripture passage. Read the passage below and then answer the questions to take a closer look at some of the details of the passage.

Isaiah by Salvatore Revelli © Only Fabrizio / shutterstock.com

Listen to me, O islands, and pay attention, you peoples from afar.
The LORD called me from the womb,
from the body of my mother he named my name.
He made my mouth like a sharp sword, in the shadow of his hand he hid me;
he made me a polished arrow, in his quiver he hid me away.
And he said to me, "You are my servant, Israel, in whom I will be glorified."
But I said, "I have labored in vain, I have spent my strength for nothing and vanity; yet surely my right is with the LORD, and my recompense with my God."

And now the LORD says,
who formed me from the womb to be his servant,
to bring Jacob back to him, and that Israel might be gathered to him,
for I am honored in the eyes of the LORD,
and my God has become my strength—
he says: "It is too light a thing that you should be my servant to raise up the tribes of Jacob and to restore the preserved of Israel; I will give you as a light to the nations, that my salvation may reach to the end of the earth."

Thus says the LORD,
the Redeemer of Israel and his Holy One,
to one deeply despised, abhorred by the nations, the servant of rulers:
"Kings shall see and arise;
princes, and they shall prostrate themselves;
because of the LORD, who is faithful, the Holy One of Israel, who has chosen you."

—Isaiah 49:1–7

SESSION 5

IMITATIO CHRISTI

What things does God do for the servant?

_____

_____

What is the servant's lament?

_____

_____

What does the servant say immediately following this lament?

_____

_____

> **MEDITATIO:** *Lectio*, a close reading and rereading of Scripture, is followed by *meditatio*, a time to reflect on the Scripture passage, and to ponder the reason for particular events, descriptions, details, phrases, and even echoes from other Scripture passages that were noticed during *lectio*. Take some time now to mediate on the above verse. To help you get started, consider the following short reflection.

> At all times Christ is aware of being "the servant of the Lord" according to the prophecy of Isaiah (cf. Is 42:1; 49:3, 6; 52:13) which includes the essential content of his messianic mission, namely, his awareness of being the Redeemer of the world. From the first moment of her divine motherhood, of her union with the Son whom "the Father sent into the world, that the world might be saved through him" (cf. Jn 3:17), Mary takes her place within Christ's messianic service. It is precisely this service which constitutes the very foundation of that Kingdom in which "to serve . . . means to reign." Christ, the "Servant of the Lord," will show all people the royal dignity of service, the dignity which is joined in the closest possible way to the vocation of every person.
> —*Mulieris Dignitatem*, 5, Pope St. John Paul II

How do the actions of the LORD show his personal involvement in the life of the servant? How does God show his personal involvement in your life?

_____

_____

Pope St. John Paul II said that Jesus's fulfillment of Isaiah's prophecy of the servant reveals "the royal dignity of service, the dignity which is joined in the closest possible way to the vocation of every person." How is God calling you to live out this vocation of royal service?

_____

_____

SESSION 5　　　　　　　　　　　　　　　　　　　　IMITATIO CHRISTI

Even when he is discouraged, the servant expresses great trust in the Lord. Do you ever feel that you "have labored in vain"? What can you do to let God be your strength?

_____

_____

> **ORATIO, CONTEMPLATIO, RESOLUTIO:** Having read and meditated on today's Scripture passage, take some time to pray, bringing your thoughts to God (*oratio*) and and to be receptive to God's grace in silence (*contemplatio*). Then end your prayer by making a simple concrete resolution (*resolutio*) to respond to God's prompting of your heart in today's prayer.

_____

_____

Jesus Christ washing the feet of His apostles at the Last Supper by Boccaccino. © Restored Traditions. Used by permission.

Commit – Day 4
God at Work in You

"God created us without us: but he did not will to save us without us."
—St. Augustine

"Work out your own salvation in fear and trembling," St. Paul tells the Philippians (2:12). At first glance, this exhortation seems to throw gas on the fire of the age-old question of faith versus works. If Paul writes in several places that we are saved by faith (see Romans 3:28; 11:6; Galatians 2:16; Ephesians 2:9), why does he tell the Philippians that they must work out their salvation? If we are no longer slaves but now sons and heirs (see Galatians 4:7), what does Paul mean by telling us to proceed with "fear and trembling"?

Chalk board house rules © James Weston / shutterstock.com

The key lies in understanding our faith as a covenant relationship. A covenant makes people who are not family, part of one family; the New Covenant that Jesus establishes makes us sons and daughters of the Father. Families have household rules. The rules don't make you part of the family, but if you are part of the family you are expected to follow the rules. The same holds true for the family of God, the Church. We can't work our way into God's family, but once we have received the unmerited gift of faith and the sanctifying grace of Baptism, we are to actively participate in our salvation.

Of course, every good work we do flows out of God's grace working in us: "For God is at work in you, both to will and to work for his good pleasure" (Philippians 2:13). Not only the good things that we do but the very desire to do good comes from God. After all, "Every good endowment and every perfect gift is from above" (James 1:17). This means that our good works really do have merit before God because God has chosen to involve us in the process of our salvation (see CCC 2008). God gets first credit for our good works because we can only do them by his grace, but he gives us credit for them too because we freely choose to cooperate with his grace.

"Justification establishes cooperation between God's grace and man's freedom. On man's part it is expressed by the assent of faith to the Word of God, which invites him to conversion, and in the cooperation of charity with the prompting of the Holy Spirit who precedes and preserves his assent:

'When God touches man's heart through the illumination of the Holy Spirit, man himself is not inactive while receiving that inspiration, since he could reject it; and yet, without God's grace, he cannot by his own free will move himself toward justice in God's sight.'" (Council of Trent (1547): DS 1525).

—CCC 1993

Consider the weight of the responsibility God has allowed us to bear: because of the reality of free will, our choices truly have eternal significance. What kinds of things do you do to "work out" your own salvation? Why do you think Paul tells us to do this with "fear and trembling"?

_____

_____

Good works demonstrate that God's gift of salvation is making an actual change in our lives. In Galatians 2:20, Paul says: "It is no longer I who live, but Christ who lives in me." In regard to working out our salvation, we might also say, "It is not I who work, but Christ who works in me." When we look at it this way, the polemical pitting of faith against works proves to be a false dichotomy. True faith will necessarily bear the visible fruit of good works. As the late singer and songwriter Rich Mullins put it, "Faith without works / is like a song you can't sing / it's about as useless as a screen door on a submarine."

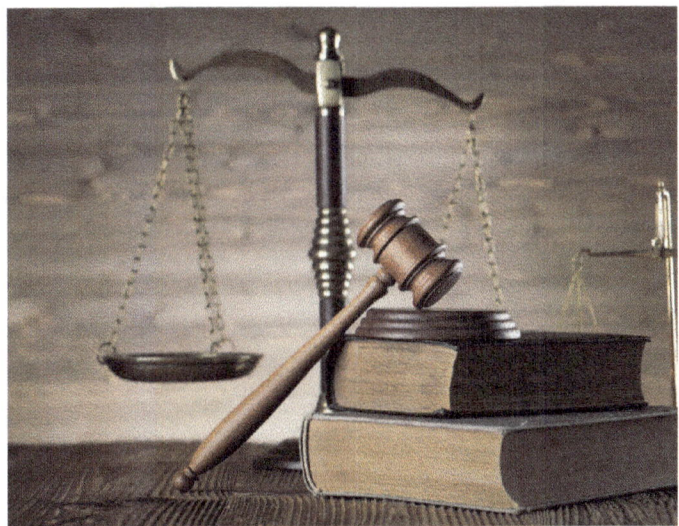

Golden scales of justice, gavel, and books. © Zoinierek / shutterstock.com

Read Hebrews 10:23–25. Who stirs you up to love and good works? Who in your life needs your encouragement in this way?

_____

_____

Commit – Day 5
Truth and Beauty

Christ Carrying the Cross,
Titian, ca. 1565, Prado Museum, Madrid

Our Lord Jesus Christ carries His cross to Mount Calvary in this art by Titian © Restored Traditions. Used by permission.

Tiziano Vecelli (or Vecellio), known in English as Titian, was one of the most important Italian painters of the sixteenth-century Venetian school. He was an incredibly versatile painter, equally skilled in portraits, landscape backgrounds, and mythological and religious subjects. Titian painted several representations of Christ carrying his Cross. The image that we reflect on today is one of a couple requested by King Philip II of Spain which now resides in Madrid's Prado Museum. A copy of this painting, by Titian's own hand, also survives and is today housed in the State Hermitage Museum, St. Petersburg.

The Gospels give us very little detail about Jesus carrying his Cross to Calvary. St. John simply says, "So they took Jesus, and he went out, bearing his own cross" (John 19:17). However, along

SESSION 5

IMITATIO CHRISTI

the route from the praetorium to Calvary, the other three Gospels attest to one particular encounter as Jesus carries his Cross. Look up the following verses. How do they describe the encounter with Simon of Cyrene?

Matthew 27:32 _____

Mark 15:20–22 _____

Luke 23:26 _____

Luke describes Simon as being "seized," and Matthew and Mark tell us that Simon was "compelled" to assist Jesus in carrying his Cross. We can imagine Simon and his sons making their way from the country into the city of Jerusalem for the Passover feast, when they unexpectedly meet the crowd following the Roman spectacle as it moved through the streets. Likely Simon hoped to avoid any involvement, but then Jesus, weak from enduring the pain and blood loss of his horrific scourging, is unable to go any further. Not wanting Jesus to expire before reaching Calvary, the soldiers pick the first man they see, Simon. Simon must have initially resisted, but the soldiers, likely with sword or spear in hand, compel him to pick up the Cross of Christ.

In an instant, Simon encounters the Son of Man, Jesus who is the Christ, the Messiah whose coming God's people so eagerly awaited. Their eyes meet, and Simon's life is forever changed. There is a tradition according to which Simon, after carrying the Cross, converted with his sons to the Faith of Christ. Thus, St. Mark adds that he was the father of Alexander and Rufus, who at the time that St. Mark wrote, must have been known disciples of Christ.

The image of Christ bearing his Cross along the road to Calvary was common in Renaissance painting. Numerous paintings exist showing Jesus either as an isolated figure carrying his Cross, or with an executioner assailing him, or accompanied by soldiers, curious bystanders, and followers (Simon among them). Exceptional, however, until Titian, are compositions featuring only Jesus and Simon the Cyrenian. The earliest surviving example (c. 1560) was the first of the two images requested by Philip II for his private chapel in the monastery of El Escorial, thus suggesting that the subject was an invention of Titian at the suggestion of the king.

With this new representation, there is no crowd, no soldiers, no road upon which Christ is walking, or place to which he is approaching. Titian puts us right up next to Jesus and the wood of the Cross, and he turns Jesus's face to look directly at us, just like he looked at Simon. We see the tears on Jesus's face. We see the blood as the thorns pierce Jesus's forehead. We see the rope around his neck. We see the nails that hold the crossbeams together, which remind us of the nails that will soon pierce Jesus's hands and feet. Jesus looks directly at us. His eyes pierce our soul, as he invites us to be his disciples and to pick up our cross and follow him (see Matthew 16:24).

It is possible that the image of Simon of Cyrene in this painting is a portrait of a man whose family had close ties to Titian (and possibly the one who commissioned the second copy of this work, which now resides in the State Hermitage Museum). Simon was most often portrayed as a peasant, but Titian's Cyrenian appears in a dark blue jacket, with a rich red collared vest, a clean white ruffled shirt, and a jeweled ring on his right thumb, all indications of a possible portrait rather than a generic image. Upon receiving the painting, Titian's model would have been able to visualize his own commitment to Christ, and would have been challenged to renew his desire to pick up his own cross each day, to share and ease Christ's suffering. If this is the case, Titian allows us to put ourselves in Simon's place. Just as Titian's model takes the place of Simon in the painting, we too can visualize ourselves taking the place of Simon in this scene, close to our Lord, sharing in Christ's suffering, just as Paul exhorted the Philippians, so that we too might also become like Christ in his death (see Philippians 3:10).

Take a moment to journal your ideas, questions, or insights about this lesson. Write down thoughts you had that may not have been mentioned in the text or the discussion questions. List any personal applications you got from the lessons. What challenged you the most in the teachings? How might you turn what you've learned into specific action?

_____
_____
_____
_____
_____
_____
_____
_____
_____
_____
_____
_____
_____
_____
_____

SESSION 6

ALL THINGS IN CHRIST

OPENING PRAYER

Glorious Saint Paul,
Most zealous apostle,
Martyr for the love of Christ,
Give us a deep faith,
A steadfast hope,
A burning love for our Lord,
So that we can proclaim with you,
"It is no longer I who live,
But Christ who lives in me."

Help us to become apostles,
Serving the Church with a pure heart,
Witnesses to her truth and beauty
Amidst the darkness of our days.
With you we praise God our Father:
"To him be the glory, in the Church
And in Christ,
Now and forever."
Amen.

—Prayer to the Apostle St. Paul,
for the Jubilee Year of St. Paul (2008–2009)

INTRODUCTION

Having described Christ's self-offering and shown himself, Timothy, and Epaphroditus as examples of disciples who model the life of Christ, Paul now calls on the Philippians (and us) to model the life of Christ in their own lives. As St. Paul closes out his letter, we'll see him reiterate the mindset that the Philippians will need to live out their heavenly citizenship and be true disciples of Christ in the midst of a pagan culture.

Connect

Do you have a personal hero or someone you look up to? Why do you admire that person? How do you show your admiration?

What are you most grateful for in your life? How do you thank God for these gifts?

Think of a time when you or someone close to you may have experienced great peace and joy in the midst of suffering. How were you or they able to maintain that peace and joy?

Video

Watch the video segment. Use the outline below to follow along and take notes.

I. Philippians 3:17–21
    A. *Typos*—mark out, model
    B. Life of Christ looks different modeled in different people (business man, mother, etc.); litmus test is not seeking self
    C. "Belly"; euphemism for sex; minds set on flesh (Romans 8)
    D. Our citizenship is in Heaven

II. Philippians 4
    A. "Agree"; *phronein* . . . be of same mind
    B. Patience/forbearance
    C. Gratitude, a fundamental habit of the mind for Christian mindset
    D. God is good Creator; "Whatever is true . . . think about these things"

SESSION 6 — ALL THINGS IN CHRIST

E. Paul's abandonment to God: key to happiness in good and bad
F. "Share"; *synkoinonia* . . . partner in my suffering
G. Business language: to your (spiritual) credit
H. Temple language: fragrant offering
I. "My" God; now "our" God
J. Our money, time, etc., are sacrifices we offer up; a pleasing aroma
K. Philippians have given; Paul praying that God gives them grace

III. Final Overview
A. Christian dual citizenship: Rome/country, plus greater citizenship of Heaven
B. We are in a venture to expand kingdom of God
C. Paul strategic in his evangelization; uses whatever is good
D. Joy is tone/tenor of letter; joy is a litmus test of our spiritual life

DISCUSS

1. What was one thing you heard for the first time or that was an "aha" moment or a challenge for you?

2. Dr. Gray described "not seeking self" as the litmus test of whether the life of Christ is being modeled in one's life. What might this look like in the life of different people (business man/woman, parent, friend, student, etc.)? How have you passed or failed this litmus test lately in your life?

3. Share something you have encountered recently that was "true, or honorable, or just, or pure, or lovely, or gracious, or excellent, or worthy of praise" (see Philippians 4:8). How did this encourage your life in Christ?

SESSION 6 — ALL THINGS IN CHRIST

4. How does abandonment to God's will help us experience true joy in our lives?

_____
_____

MEMORY VERSE

"I can do all things in him who strengthens me."

—Philippians 4:13

CLOSING PRAYER

Let us pray with the words of St. Paul from his Letter to the Philippians:

Rejoice in the Lord always; again I will say, Rejoice.
Let all men know [our] forbearance. The Lord is at hand.
Have no anxiety about anything, but in everything by prayer
and supplication with thanksgiving let [our] requests be made known to God.
And the peace of God, which passes all understanding,
will keep [our] hearts and [our] minds in Christ Jesus.
Amen.

St. Paul, Apostle of the Crucified Lord, pray for us.

FOR FURTHER READING

Catechism of the Catholic Church, 1803–1809 ("The Virtues")

Pope Paul VI, *Lumen Gentium (The Dogmatic Constitution on the Church),* 50

St. Louis de Montfort, *Letter to the Friends of the Cross*

Commit—Day 1
Imitation

Imitation, or *mimesis*, is the pedagogical foundation for the Greek ideal of education. Plato/Socrates noted that through *mimesis* a youth would ultimately develop not only the habits but also the nature of the teacher's body, voice and thinking. Aristotle also recognized the natural impulse in human beings, from childhood onward, to imitate what we see, noting that because of this we learn first by imitation. The importance of imitation for Greek education is seen in the numerous written works on the lives of important men—written so that the deeds of such figures might be imitated. Plutarch, in his *Lives*, notes that it is acts of virtue in particular that stir a reader to imitation; that acts of virtue create at once both admiration of the things done and desire to imitate the doers of them. Thus for the Greeks the expectation was that as the pupil imitated what they saw and heard, these imitations would pass into character.

Father shaving in the mirror. Kid son imitates father © Oksana Kuzmina / shutterstock.com

The Christian classical application of is built on this Greek foundation and it is understood that while some virtues are infused by Divine grace, others are acquired by practicing the acts of virtue, often in imitation of others. This imitation is not lifeless but is driven by, and is the fruit of, love—the love of God in Christ Jesus. Each of us is called to holiness, exhorted by Scripture to be holy as the Lord God is holy (Leviticus 20:26). However God, in his goodness, does not leave us to our own devices. He sets before us holy examples, with the ultimate example being that of his Son, Jesus Christ, who gave his life for us and calls us to follow him for he is the "way, the truth and the life" (John 14:6).

In addition to our Lord, the Scriptures continually set before us the lives of holy men and women—both by recounting the narrative stories of their lives and deeds, and by enumerating lists of these righteous individuals (see Sirach 44-50 and Hebrews 11). In his various letters, Paul often encourages the faithful to imitate him and his companions. Look up the following Scripture passages. What does Paul call us to imitate?

1 Corinthians 4:9–17 _____

_____

Philippians 3:17 _____

_____

1 Thessalonians 2:9–14 _____

_____

89

Cain and Abel by Ghiberti. © Timur Kulgarin / shutterstock.com

Jesus Christ also gives us his Church to guide us on the path to holiness, and in that Church we have a "great cloud of witnesses" who have followed Christ faithfully and gone before us. The Church has honored the saints since the earliest days. In the beginning, special veneration was reserved for the martyrs but was expanded in the fourth century to those "confessors" who suffered but did not die for their faith. St. Thomas Aquinas describes that we who are on our way to eternal happiness are led to it by words and examples, and this is the reason why we celebrate the feasts of the saints who have already attained happiness, so that we may be built up by their examples and stimulated by their reward.

The following excerpt from the Vatican II document, *Lumen Gentium*, promulgated by Pope Paul VI, reminds us of the Church's long history of and purpose in the veneration of saints:

> When we look at the lives of those who have faithfully followed Christ, we are inspired with a new reason for seeking the City that is to come and at the same time we are shown a most safe path by which among the vicissitudes of this world, in keeping with the state in life and condition proper to each of us, we will be able to arrive at perfect union with Christ, that is, perfect holiness. In the lives of those who, sharing in our humanity, are however more perfectly transformed into the image of Christ, God vividly manifests His presence and His face to men. He speaks to us in them, and gives us a sign of His Kingdom, to which we are strongly drawn, having so great a cloud of witnesses over us and such a witness to the truth of the Gospel.
>
> –*Lumen Gentium*, 50

Do you have a favorite saint? If so, why did you choose this particular saint? If not, consult a resource such as Butler's *Lives of the Saints* or look up saints online to help you identify a saint who can be an additional model for you of how to more faithfully live out the life of Christ. End today's reflection by praying to this saint for their intercession.

_____

_____

_____

Commit–Day 2
Friends of the Cross

St. Louis de Montfort is a seventeenth-century priest renowned for his devotion to the Blessed Virgin Mary and for his fidelity to the Cross of Christ. De Montfort's passionate love for the Cross is manifested in his *Letter to the Friends of the Cross*. Written to an association of his most ardent followers who likewise wished to espouse the Cross, his letter is the fruit of a weeklong retreat immersed in meditation on and communion with the Crucified Savior and his Blessed Mother. Although written more than two hundred years ago, the letter remains a fresh clarion call to wage war against the evils of secularism and materialism of modern society. It reminds us that the pathway to holiness still passes by way of Christ, for he is "the way, the truth and the life" (John 14:6) and him crucified (see 1 Corinthians 2:2).

Following his admonishment and exposition that the path to holiness necessarily demands we follow Christ, renounce ourselves, and pick up our cross, de Montfort reminds us that mere suffering is not sufficient by itself. Jesus invites us to follow him, that is, to suffer the way he did. In the words of St. Peter, "to this you have been called, because Christ also suffered for you, leaving you an example, that you should follow in his steps" (1 Peter 2:21).

Jesus Christ carrying the Holy Cross on a vintage background © nito/ shutterstock.com

The letter closes with fourteen rules to aid us in following in the footsteps of Christ. As you read and reflect on these rules, consider the crosses that you may be currently carrying and how St. Louis de Montfort's rules can assist you in following our Lord more closely.

The Fourteen Rules

1. *Not to deliberately cause crosses, by one's own fault: Do not deliberately contrive to bring crosses upon yourself . . .*

2. *Be aware of one's neighbor's good: If you happen to do something which is neither good nor bad in itself, and your neighbor takes scandal at it—although without reason—refrain from doing it, out of charity to him . . .*

3. *Admire the sublime virtue of the saints without pretending to attain to it: . . . let us be content with admiring and praising the marvelous work of the Holy Spirit in their souls . . .*

5th Station of the Cross, Simon of Cyrene carries the cross
© Zvonimir Atletic / shutterstock.com

4. **Ask God for the wisdom of the Cross:** . . . *that knowledge of the truth which we experience within ourselves and which by the light of faith deepens our knowledge of the most hidden mysteries, including that of the Cross* . . .

5. **Humble oneself for one's faults, without worrying:** . . . *If there is anything wrong in what you have done, accept the humiliation as a punishment for it; if it was not sinful, accept it as a means of humbling your pride* . . .

6. **God humbles us to purify us:** . . . *Oh, how wonderful is God in his saints, and in the means he adopts to lead them to humility and holiness!*

7. **Avoid the trap of pride in one's crosses:** *Do not be like those proud and self-conceited church-goers, imagining that your crosses are heavy, that they are proofs of your fidelity and marks of God's exceptional love for you* . . .

8. **Profit by little sufferings rather than great ones:** . . . *God considers not so much what we suffer as how we suffer . . . to suffer little or much for God's sake is to suffer like a saint.*

9. **Love crosses, not with an emotional love, but with rational and supernatural love:** . . . *God does not ask you to love the Cross with the will of the flesh . . . [Rational] love is entirely spiritual; it springs from the knowledge of how happy we can be in suffering for God, and so it can experienced by the soul, to which it gives interior joy and strength . . . And so there is a third kind of love, which is called by the masters of the spiritual life the love of the summit of the soul, and which is known to philosophers as the love of the intellect. In this, without any feeling of joy in the senses or pleasure in the mind, we love the cross we are carrying, by the light of pure faith, and take delight in it . . . It is with one of these two higher loves that we should love and accept the Cross.*

10. **Suffer all sorts of crosses, without exception and without choice:** *My dear Friends of the Cross, make the resolution to suffer any kind of cross without excluding or choosing any* . . .

11. **Four considerations for suffering well:** *To help you suffer in the right spirit, acquire the good habit of reflecting on these four points:*
    - *The eye of God: [looks with pleasure on] the one who is struggling with the world, the devil, and himself for the love of God, the one who carries his cross cheerfully* . . .
    - *The hand of God: All natural evils which befall us, from the smallest to the greatest, come from the hand of God.*
    - *The wounds and sufferings of Christ crucified:* . . . *Look with the eyes of your body, and see through the eyes of your contemplation, whether your poverty, destitution, disgrace, sorrow, desolation are like mine; look upon me who am innocent, and lament, you who are guilty!* . . .
    - *Heaven above; Hell below: Look upwards and see the beautiful crown that awaits you in heaven if you carry your cross well . . . Now let us look downward to the place we have deserved* . . .

12. **Never complain against creatures:** *Never complain against any person or thing that God may use to afflict you.*

SESSION 6

ALL THINGS IN CHRIST

13. *Accept the Cross only with gratitude: . . . always welcome it with humility and gratitude.*

14. *Take up some voluntary crosses: If you want to make yourself worthy of the best kind of crosses, that is, those which come to you without your choosing, then under the guidance of a prudent director, take up some of your own accord . . .*

Take some time today to thank God for the crosses he has allowed you to carry. Write down some ways that you can be a better "Friend of the Cross."

_____

_____

_____

12th Stations of the Cross, Jesus dies on the cross. © Zvonimir Atletic / shutterstock.com

Commit – Day 3
Lectio: Think on These Things

As St. Paul prepares to close his letter to his beloved brethren in the church at Philippi, he exhorts them to live lives of prayer and contemplation of all that is virtuous. Paul challenges the Philippians to driveced out any unworthy or impure thoughts by filling their minds with what is good, true, and beautiful. Let's take a closer look at this exhortation to consider how we also might benefit from his counsel.

Saint Paul painting from Paris - St. Severin church © Renata Sedmakova / shutterstock.com

> **LECTIO:** The practice of praying with Scripture, *lectio divina*, begins with an active and close reading of the Scripture passage. Read the passage below and then answer the questions to take a closer look at some of the details of the passage.

Finally, brethren, whatever is true, whatever is honorable, whatever is just, whatever is pure, whatever is lovely, whatever is gracious, if there is any excellence, if there is anything worthy of praise, think about these things.
—Philippians 4:8

What six adjectives follow Paul's words "whatever is . . ."?

_____

_____

What two nouns follow "if there is . . ."?

_____

_____

What does Paul ask of the Philippians?

_____

_____

SESSION 6

ALL THINGS IN CHRIST

> **MEDITATIO:** *Lectio*, a close reading and rereading of Scripture, is followed by *meditatio*, a time to reflect on the Scripture passage, and to ponder the reason for particular events, descriptions, details, phrases, and even echoes from other Scripture passages that were noticed during *lectio*. Take some time now to mediate on the above verse. To help you get started, consider the following short reflection.

What is more, Saint Francis, faithful to Scripture, invites us to see nature as a magnificent book in which God speaks to us and grants us a glimpse of his infinite beauty and goodness. "Through the greatness and the beauty of creatures one comes to know by analogy their maker" (Wis 13:5); indeed, "his eternal power and divinity have been made known through his works since the creation of the world" (Rom 1:20). For this reason, Francis asked that part of the friary garden always be left untouched, so that wild flowers and herbs could grow there, and those who saw them could raise their minds to God, the Creator of such beauty. Rather than a problem to be solved, the world is a joyful mystery to be contemplated with gladness and praise.

—Pope Francis, *Laudato Si'*, 12

Sunrise on Yosemite Valley, Yosemite National Park, California © Stephen Moehle / shutterstock.com

Paul tells us in his letter to the Romans that the invisible Creator can be clearly discerned in the beauty and harmony of his creation. Read the creation account in Genesis 1. What adjective does God apply to what he has created each day? Why is it important to remember this about God's creation?

_____

_____

_____

_____

Why does Paul want the Philippians, and us, to think about the good? For what purpose?

_____

_____

Meditatio often includes reflecting on Scripture in light of other Scripture verses. Consider how Paul's six adjectives describe Jesus Christ. Then consider how you can further develop this virtue in your own life (some examples or admonitions are provided to help get you started).

Jesus on the cross in vestibule of church in Vienna. © Renata Sedmakova / shutterstock.com

Adjective	Scripture Verse	What is the Connection to Jesus?	Living It in My Life
True	Matthew 22:16 John 1:9 John 6:32 John 8:14 John 15:1, 5		John 3:21; 4:23; 7:18
Honorable	James 2:7		1 Peter 2:12
Just	John 5:30 Acts 22:14		Matthew 7:12
Pure	1 John 3:3		Matthew 5:8
Lovely	John 15:13		1 Corinthians 13:4–7
Gracious	Luke 4:22		Isaiah 30:18 Psalm 116:5

> **ORATIO, CONTEMPLATIO, RESOLUTIO:** Having read and meditated on today's Scripture passage, take some time to pray, bringing your thoughts to God (*oratio*) and and to be receptive to God's grace in silence (*contemplatio*). Then end your prayer by making a simple concrete resolution (*resolutio*) to respond to God's prompting of your heart in today's prayer.

Commit–Day 4
All Things in Christ

The final chapter of Paul's letter is a recapitulation of several themes expounded upon earlier in the letter. Recall that Paul's primary purpose in addressing the Philippians is to encourage them to continue their spiritual growth through imitation of both Jesus Christ, their Savior, and Paul, their father in the faith. By emulating these two central figures, the Philippians can learn to accept their crosses with humility and patient endurance. Let's look closely at these final verses in order to gain a more complete understanding of how Paul summarizes the major themes of his letter.

Looking at verse 4:1 and recalling Paul's appeal in verse 1:27, what does Paul want the Philippians to do? How are they to accomplish this? Why do you think that Paul begins his final exhortation with this reminder?

_____
_____

Next, in verses 4:2–3, Paul addresses two specific women, calling them to resolve their differences. How does Paul appeal to the theme of partnership first mentioned in 1:5?

_____
_____
_____
_____
_____

Strategic Partnership concept on the gearwheels © AlexLMX / shutterstock.com

Paul repeats the key word "rejoice" in verse 4:4. Why is this concept so important for the Philippians to understand (see also 1:19)?

_____
_____

Paul turns to prayer as the source of peace in the lives of followers of Christ in verses 5–7. They are to live in consideration of others and be assured that Christ is ever near to them. How can they allay any anxiety about their circumstances? What does Paul remind them is the fruit of prayer?

_____
_____

SESSION 6 ALL THINGS IN CHRIST

At this point, we return to the virtues from our Commit Day 3 *lectio* that Paul asks the Philippians to reflect upon. In the following (verse 9), Paul reminds them of a further means of experiencing God's peace in their lives. What does Paul remind them to do?

_____
_____

In verse 4:10, Paul again expresses his joy in the Lord for the Philippians and their concern for him. Although he remains imprisoned, he does not complain about his circumstances because he has learned how to be content (verse 11). To what or whom does Paul attribute this ability to remain detached from physical comfort and consolation? See 4:13.

_____
_____

Paul is grateful to the Philippians for their care and support. What underlying truth does Dr. Gray explain in the video as the basis for their support? See 4:14–15.

_____
_____

Good Friday procession, St. Joseph church, Ft. Collins, CO © Augustine Institute. All rights reserved.

In 4:17–19, Paul assures the Philippians that although he is thankful, he does not seek the gift from them but, rather, he hopes that their generosity should return to them. In what terms does Paul describe the gift the Philippians sent to him via Epaphroditus? And how does he hope God will respond to their generosity?

_____
_____

Paul then concludes his letter with the typical greetings and the final doxology: "The grace of the Lord Jesus Chris be with your spirit."

SESSION 6

ALL THINGS IN CHRIST

Close-up of woman's hands while reading the Bible outside. © Prixel Creative / shutterstock.com

By closely reading the Scriptures and reflecting upon them we can enter more deeply into the message they contain. In his closing exhortation, Paul returns to the major themes spoken throughout his letter (peace and joy, partnership, imitation of Christ, and their citizenship in Heaven). Paul desires the Philippians, whom he loves and whom are his partners in the Gospel, to remember who they are in Christ and live lives worthy of the gospel in order that the good work begun in them will be brought "to completion at the day of Jesus Christ" (Philippians 1:6).

Commit – Day 5
Truth and Beauty

The Christian Martyrs' Last Prayer,
Jean-Léon Gérôme, c. 1863–1883, Walters Art Gallery, Baltimore

The Christian Martyrs' Last Prayer art by Jean-Léon Gérôme © Restored Traditions. Used by permission.

In 1863 William T. Walters commissioned Jean-Léon Gérôme to paint *The Christian Martyrs' Last Prayer*. After 20 years and three re-paintings, Gérôme delivered the finished picture, considering it among his most important works.

In a letter to Walters, Gérôme identified the setting as the Circus Maximus (even though the stadium seating appears to more closely resemble that of the Colosseum). The Circus Maximus was Rome's racecourse, and Gérôme shows us the center goal posts around which the horses and chariots turned, leaving deep tracks in the sandy floor as the chariots chased one another during their seven-lap race. Rome's circuses and amphitheaters were home to the *ludi circenses*, the circus games, which included chariot races, gladiatorial competitions, wild beast hunts, public executions, and even sea battles.

Gérôme places us in Nero's Rome, hinted at by the shadowed statue and buildings that tower beyond the circus and recall Nero's grand Golden House built on the Palatine Hill and the nearly 100 foot colossal bronze statue of himself that stood in its courtyard. After the Great Fire of Rome in AD 64 conveniently consumed much of the city center, Nero used this land to build his lavish imperial residence, which overlooked an enormous man-made lake. As rumors persisted that Nero may have been responsible for the fire and the resulting hardship of the Roman people, Nero shielded himself from the growing accusations by blaming the Christians for the devastation and initiated the empire's first Christian persecution. The Roman historian Tacitus, in his *Annals*, recounts some of what the Christians suffered:

First those were seized who admitted their faith, and then, using the information they provided, a vast multitude were convicted, not so much for the crime of burning the city, but for hatred of the human race. And perishing they were additionally made into sports: they were killed by dogs by having the hides of beasts attached to them, or they were nailed to crosses or set aflame, and, when the daylight passed away, they were used as nighttime lamps.

—Tacitus, *Annals*

Gérôme transports us to one of Nero's evening circus persecutions, not as spectators amongst the Roman crowd, but by dropping us onto the circus floor with the men and women facing martyrdom. At first glance, it is easy for the viewer to lose sight of the Christian martyrs with the enormity of the circus stadium all around. But this perspective helps the viewer empathize with this small group of men and women who find themselves surrounded by a massive, hostile, jeering crowd of 150,000 or more, who lust for their blood and death.

A trap door opens, and the first wild beasts make their way from the underground darkness into the evening twilight. Human torches are already being lit to illuminate this last horrifying spectacle of the day. One might expect terror to overcome the small band of believers, sending them fleeing in all directions from the approaching beasts. Instead their focus is turned heavenward as they kneel, heads bowed, likely led in prayer by the elder, or presbyter, who stands in the midst of the group.

Such a reaction, in the face of terrible suffering and martyrdom, does not come naturally, but is the fruit of having the mind of Christ and striving to imitate the life of Christ. Look up the following verses. What model did Jesus give to follow?

Matthew 26:36–39 _____

Luke 23:33–37 _____

Later it would be the witness of these first martyrs that would strengthen other Christians when they too faced persecutions in their own time. Christians like St. Ignatius of Antioch who wrote letters to seven churches as he was being transported to Rome for his martyrdom. In his letter to the church at Rome he wrote:

Only request in my behalf both inward and outward strength, that I may not only speak, but [truly] will; and that I may not merely be called a Christian, but really be found to be one . . . I write to the Churches, and impress on them all, that I shall willingly die for God, unless ye hinder me. I beseech of you not to show an unseasonable good-will towards me. Suffer me to become food for the wild beasts, through whose instrumentality it will be granted me to attain to God. I am the wheat of God, and let me be ground by the teeth of the wild beasts, that I may be found the pure bread of Christ. Rather entice the wild beasts, that they may become my tomb, and may leave nothing of my body; so that when I have fallen asleep [in death], I may be no trouble to any one. Then shall I truly be a disciple of Christ, when the world shall not see so much as my body. Entreat Christ for me, that by these instruments I may be found a sacrifice [to God].

—Saint Ignatius of Antioch

SESSION 6 ALL THINGS IN CHRIST

That Ignatius of Antioch could write such words, and the early Christian martyrs could offer their lives with such peace and joy, is something that makes one pause in wonder. Even the first lion upon the circus floor in Gérôme's painting appears to be transfixed, amazed to find such faith upon the earth.

Take a moment to journal your ideas, questions, or insights about this lesson. Write down thoughts you had that may not have been mentioned in the text or the discussion questions. List any personal applications you got from the lessons. What challenged you the most in the teachings? How might you turn what you've learned into specific action?

_____
_____
_____
_____
_____
_____
_____
_____
_____
_____
_____
_____
_____
_____
_____
_____